Tableau®

FOR

DUMMIES®

A Wiley Brand

Tableau®

FOR DUMMIES®

A Wiley Brand

by Molly Monsey and Paul Sochan

FOR DUMMIES®
A Wiley Brand

Tableau® For Dummies®

Published by: **John Wiley & Sons, Inc.,** 111 River Street, Hoboken, NJ 07030-5774, www.wiley.com

Copyright © 2016 by John Wiley & Sons, Inc., Hoboken, New Jersey

Published simultaneously in Canada

No part of this publication may be reproduced, stored in a retrieval system, or transmitted in any form or by any means, electronic, mechanical, photocopying, recording, scanning or otherwise, except as permitted under Sections 107 or 108 of the 1976 United States Copyright Act, without the prior written permission of the Publisher. Requests to the Publisher for permission should be addressed to the Permissions Department, John Wiley & Sons, Inc., 111 River Street, Hoboken, NJ 07030, (201) 748-6011, fax (201) 748-6008, or online at http://www.wiley.com/go/permissions.

Trademarks: Wiley, For Dummies, the Dummies Man logo, Dummies.com, Making Everything Easier, and related trade dress are trademarks or registered trademarks of John Wiley & Sons, Inc., and may not be used without written permission. Tableau is a registered trademark of Tableau Software, Inc. All other trademarks are the property of their respective owners. John Wiley & Sons, Inc., is not associated with any product or vendor mentioned in this book.

For general information on our other products and services, please contact our Customer Care Department within the U.S. at 877-762-2974, outside the U.S. at 317-572-3993, or fax 317-572-4002. For technical support, please visit www.wiley.com/techsupport.

Wiley publishes in a variety of print and electronic formats and by print-on-demand. Some material included with standard print versions of this book may not be included in e-books or in print-on-demand. If this book refers to media such as a CD or DVD that is not included in the version you purchased, you may download this material at http://booksupport.wiley.com. For more information about Wiley products, visit www.wiley.com.

Library of Congress Control Number: 2015952179

ISBN: 978-1-119-13479-4; 978-1-119-13483-1 (ebk); 978-1-119-13491-6 (ebk)

Manufactured in the United States of America

10 9 8 7 6 5 4 3 2 1

Contents at a Glance

Table of Contents

Introduction

· ·

Data analysis and data visualization are vital in today's extremely competitive business climate. But doing great analysis and creating useful visualizations can feel difficult, complex, and not for the faint of heart. Fortunately, a solution is available that makes the whole process much easier and will have you analyzing and visualizing data like a pro in no time. Tableau Desktop is a tool that was designed to enable you to perform complex data analysis tasks and create powerful, interactive visualizations that communicate the analysis. In addition, Tableau allows you to share your analysis and visualizations across your organization, so everyone from coworkers to top management can dig into the data that matters to them. This truly is a tool that provides you with a huge competitive advantage.

About This Book

In the past, most people got along with using tools like Microsoft Excel to analyze business data. Although there's no getting around the fact that Excel is both popular and useful, Tableau provides a significant boost in power and ease-of-use when it comes to in-depth data analysis, data visualization, and communicating with data. Quite simply, you need a tool like Tableau Desktop to do the job right. *Tableau For Dummies* provides you with the introduction and information you need to make use of this tool.

Tableau For Dummies isn't the only source of information that you can find about Tableau Desktop, but we like to think that it's the easiest source you'll find, especially with our easy-access organization. We've organized this book into several parts so that you can easily find what you need.

Part I: Getting Started with Tableau Desktop

In this part, you'll get a quick look at Tableau Desktop, see what you can do with this tool, and have a brief introduction to the basics of the product. This is a great place to start, not only for new Tableau Desktop users but also for anyone who is tasked with deciding whether Tableau can fulfill the needs of your organization.

Part II: Bringing in Data

The chapters in this part help you understand the types of data that you can use with Tableau Desktop, show you how to connect to that data, and provide the basics of getting started with data visualizations.

Part III: Analyzing Data

In this part, you get a chance to dig a little bit deeper into working with Tableau Desktop. You'll see how you can use different options to create the best visualizations, how to create special interactive pages that make it easier to share your analyses, and how to tell a story that leads viewers through the analysis process.

Part IV: Publishing and Sharing

The ability to publish and share your data analysis and visualization with the other people in your organization is the subject of this part. You'll quickly see several different options so that you can choose the best one to suit your needs.

Part V: Advancing to a Higher Level

After you master the basics of Tableau Desktop, you may want to take things to a higher level; if that sounds like you, this part should be your destination. Here you'll find out about more advanced topics like filtering and calculated fields.

Part VI: The Part of Tens

We have a tradition of closing our books with some lists of ten or so items that we feel are pretty important for you to know. We give you some tips and other useful information in this part.

Conventions Used in This Book

To make things just a bit easier to understand, this book follows certain conventions that include the following:

 ✔ Bold text means that you should type the text just as it appears in the book. The exception is when you're working through a steps list: Because each step is bold, the text to type is not bold.

✔ Web addresses and programming code appear in monofont. If you're reading a digital version of this book on a device connected to the Internet, you can click the web address to visit that website, like this: `www.dummies.com`.

✔ Command sequences appear using the command arrow. For example: Choose File ⇨ Open to open a Tableau workbook.

Foolish Assumptions

For the purposes of this book, we assume that you're probably just getting started with Tableau Desktop or that you're checking out the product to see whether it fits your needs. We'll also assume that you're familiar with your computer and that you've probably tinkered around with Excel at least a little bit. You don't have to be an Excel expert, but it will be easier to grasp the power and simplicity of working with data in Tableau if you already have a basic understanding of Excel.

Icons Used in This Book

The Tip icon marks tips (duh!) and shortcuts that you can use to make using Tableau Desktop easier.

Remember icons mark the information that's especially important to know. To siphon off the most important information in each chapter, just skim through these icons.

The Technical Stuff icon marks information of a highly technical nature that you can normally skip over without losing the main thread of the discussion.

The Warning icon tells you to watch out! It marks important information that may save you headaches.

Beyond the Book

We have written a lot of extra content that you won't find in this book. Go online to find the following:

- ✔ **The Cheat Sheet for this book is at**

  www.dummies.com/cheatsheet/tableau

- ✔ **Some great bonus content, as well as any updates to this book, are at**

  http://www.dummies.com/extras/tableau

Where to Go from Here

You don't have to read this book from beginning to end if you don't want to. If you're just looking for help on a specific topic, feel free to jump to the appropriate chapter and dig in. Later, you can go back and pick up useful information in the other chapters as you need it.

If you're just thinking about whether Tableau Desktop can help you, you'll probably want to start with the first two chapters and then skim the rest of the book to see what's possible. Of course, you'll also find it very helpful to download Tableau Desktop's trial version and try out some of the examples.

Part I
Getting Started with Tableau Desktop

In this part . . .

- Discover what Tableau Desktop can do for you.
- Master the Tableau Desktop basics.

A Brief Introduction to Tableau Desktop

In This Chapter

▶ Getting started with Tableau

▶ Taking Tableau for a test drive

▶ Understanding what you're seeing

*G*etting started with any new software product can be a real adventure. Not only do you have new ways of doing things, but you also need to deal with a completely new user experience — one that maybe displays information in ways that you're not quite used to. This chapter helps introduce you to Tableau and the exciting new opportunities it presents you with for analyzing and visualizing your data.

Before you can begin using Tableau, you need to have it installed on your computer. So, we begin this chapter by showing you how to find and download a free trial version. Additionally, in this chapter we show you some of the things that you'll learn to do in Tableau. Sit back and relax. There'll be plenty of opportunities to try out the product in future chapters

Starting with Tableau

If you're like most people, you probably find it far more fun and interesting to actually try something yourself instead of simply reading about it. Fortunately, with Tableau, it's both quick and easy to download and install a trial copy of the latest full version of the software.

Downloading the Tableau trial

Before you can begin using Tableau, you'll have to pay a visit to the Tableau Software website and download the current version of the software. You'll need to register first, but you don't need to supply a credit card number, so don't worry about getting billed.

The trial version of Tableau that you download will work for 14 days, so you'll want to make sure that you have some free time in your schedule to try out the application during that trial period. You probably don't want to begin your trial just before you leave for a relaxing vacation.

To download your free Tableau trial, follow these steps:

1. **Open your web browser and visit** www.tableau.com/products/desktop **and click on "Try it Free."**

    The default version of Tableau Desktop starts to download automatically. This will be either the 64-bit Windows version or the Mac version, depending on your computer.

    If you need a different version, cancel the download and click the 32-bit Windows link or the Mac link to download one of those versions. (See Figure 1-1.)

2. **Wait for your download to complete.**

    That's pretty much it. The next section walks you through how to install your downloaded software.

Installing the trial software

After the download has completed, you can install the trial immediately or wait until later. If you don't want to install the software right now, be sure to remember where you saved the file. If you do want to install the trial now, follow these steps:

1. **Click the Run button in the dialog box that appears in order to begin the installation process.**

    If you don't install the trial immediately, locate the saved file later and run it to begin the installation.

2. **Read the license agreement and then select the check box to indicate that you've read and agree with the terms.**

    You won't be able to install the software unless you select this check box.

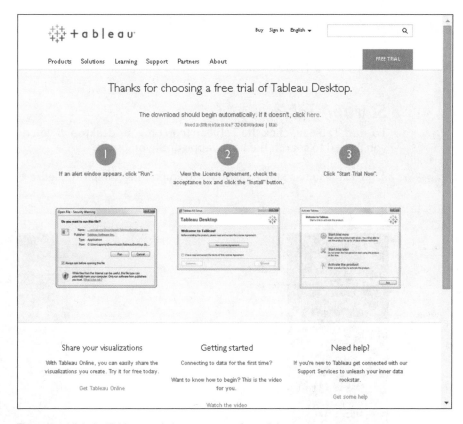

Figure 1-1: Visit the Tableau website to get your free trial.

3. **Click the Install button to continue.**

4. **After the installation completes, click the Start Trial Now link if you'd like to begin using the software.**

   You can also click the Start Trial Later link if you're not ready quite yet, or the Register Tableau link if you want to convert your copy from a trial to the fully registered version.

Depending on your computer's operating system, you might see slightly different prompts, but the general steps for downloading and installing the Tableau trial should be quite similar. You also might check the Tech Specs located on Tableau's website at www.tableau.com/products/desktop.

Looking at the Tableau Workspace

Now that you've taken care of getting the trial version installed, it's time to take a look at Tableau itself.

Starting Tableau

To start Tableau, click the Tableau icon on your desktop. If you don't find it, you'll need to search the list of apps until you find it.

After Tableau has started, you'll see something similar to Figure 1-2.

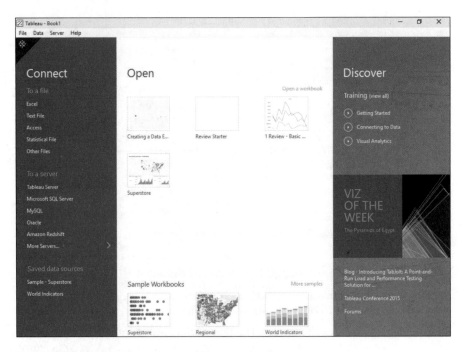

Figure 1-2: The Tableau Start page provides several options.

As Figure 1-2 shows, the Tableau Start page is divided into three main sections:

> ✔ **Connect:** This section runs down the left side of the page and gives you the option to connect to various data sources. These sources include files that are arranged in a database format as well as various types of database servers. See Chapter 4 for additional information on the types of data that you can use with Tableau.

✓ **Open:** This center section of the Start page enables you to open existing Tableau workbooks. The top part of this section shows any workbooks that you've recently opened, and the bottom part of the section provides quick access to sample workbooks that you can use to practice with Tableau.

✓ **Discover:** The right section of the Start page provides access to various Tableau training resources as well as to other interesting content such as news, blogs, and forums.

Viewing a sample workbook or data source

The best way to see what Tableau can do is to take a look at a quick example. We're not going to try and show you something complex, but rather just a simple example to whet your appetite.

You can open any of the sample workbooks by clicking one of the icons on the Start page. Additionally, the Connect section on the left offers several sample data sources you can try.

Figure 1-3 shows how Tableau might look after you've connected to a sample data source. In this case, we chose to connect using Excel under the To a File option and browsed to the location of the *Sample – Superstore* data set provided by Tableau. This sample and others are stored in a directory called "My Tableau Repository" that accompanies the Tableau Desktop download. Although it's an Excel file, Tableau will have much the same appearance regardless of the type of data source you choose. The field names listed under Dimensions and Measures in the Data pane on the left will vary according to what's actually in your data source.

The real magic happens after you drag items from the Data pane onto the workspace. In Figure 1-4, the Sales measure is being dragged onto the Rows field.

Figure 1-5 shows the result that appears after Sales is dropped. With just that one step, Tableau displays a chart showing total sales.

While this bar chart is useful to get a quick glance at our sales overall, in order to get more detailed information you'll want to add more data to the view. In Figure 1-6, the Ship Mode field was dragged to the Columns field and Tableau immediately changed the chart to display the sales for each Ship Mode.

The bar chart shown in Figure 1-6 shows useful information, allowing us to compare which Ship Mode is making the most profit. Tableau makes it easy to gain this insight and then move to explore another question. For example, in order to build the map as seen in Figure 1-7, we created a new worksheet and simply double-clicked on the geographic State field, then added Sales to Size on the Marks card.

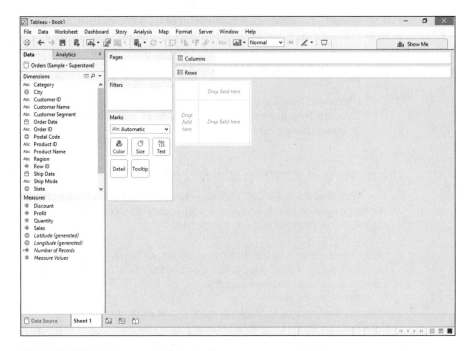

Figure 1-3: Tableau after connecting to a data source.

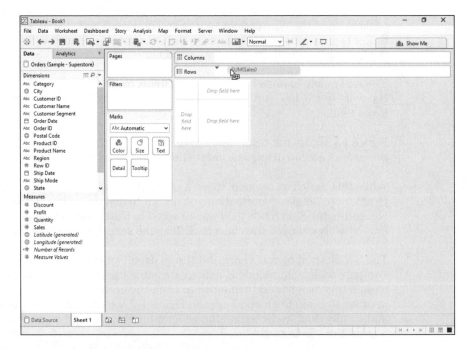

Figure 1-4: Dropping Sales onto Rows.

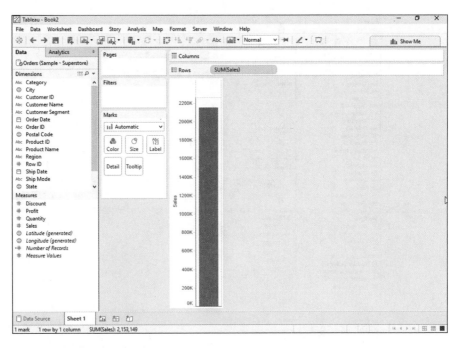

Figure 1-5: Tableau after Sales is added to Rows.

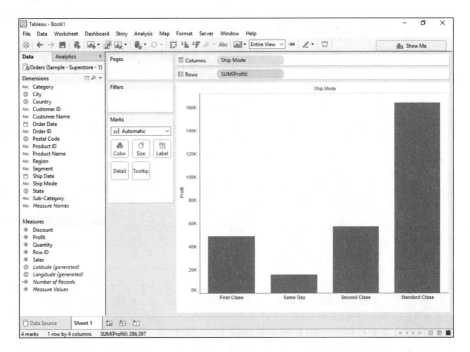

Figure 1-6: Tableau displays a much more useful chart when additional fields are added.

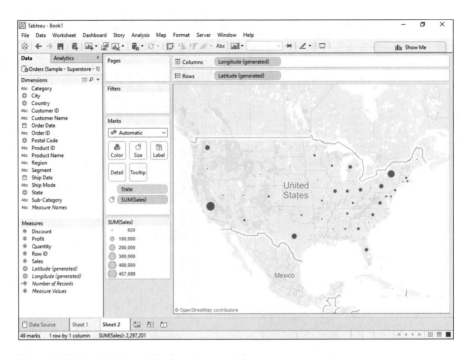

Figure 1-7: Sales data is now displayed as symbols on a map.

Seeing what Tableau can really do

Tableau worksheets are powerful analytical tools, but the real utility of this application is in being able to share the analysis with other people in your organization. An executive overview such as the one shown in Figure 1-8 not only breaks down sales by state, but it also enables the viewer to see how different customer segments and product categories are performing. In addition, the overview graphically displays profitability using different colors. In Tableau terminology, this type of display that combines information from more than one sheet is called a *dashboard*.

The Tableau dashboard shown in Figure 1-8 also includes a couple of controls in the upper-right section so that the viewer can filter the information that's displayed. For example, an executive might want to focus on profitability in a single region during the most recent year. These interactive controls make it easy for the executive to apply the filters without having any Tableau or data analysis expertise.

In Chapter 11, you'll see that Tableau has another option called *stories* that takes the dashboard concept one step further. By building a story, you can take viewers step by step through your analysis to help them better understand how you reached your conclusions.

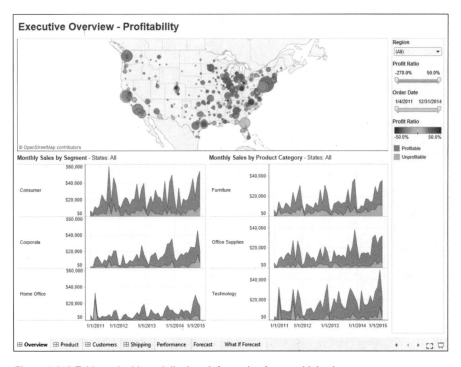

Figure 1-8: A Tableau dashboard displays information from multiple sheets.

Seeing What You Can Do with Tableau

ompanies around the world endeavor to make data-driven decisions and gain competitive advantage. However, the overly complex and outdated tools of the past are now making users restless and frustrated. In this chapter, you will see how Tableau enables you to have a conversation with your data, leading to powerful analysis and quicker insight for easier real-time decision making.

Analyzing Data

People have a hard time getting much useful information from raw data until they perform some sort of data analysis on the numbers. In the past, it was fairly common to simply do some magic and produce numbers that summarized the data and call the job complete. Today, executives expect their staff to go well beyond simply producing reports that summarize data numerically. People want insightful graphical representations that make it easier to understand the results of the data analysis.

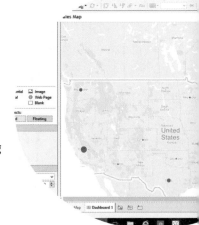

Looking back at data analysis

Traditionally, you probably used something like Excel (or maybe Access) to do data analysis. For example, Figure 2-1 shows an Excel worksheet that contains sales results for a sample chain of stores. In terms of analyzing this data in Excel, about the only good thing you can say is that the information is organized so that each row contains the record of one sale and each column contains the data for one field. The next step of analyzing the data can be challenging.

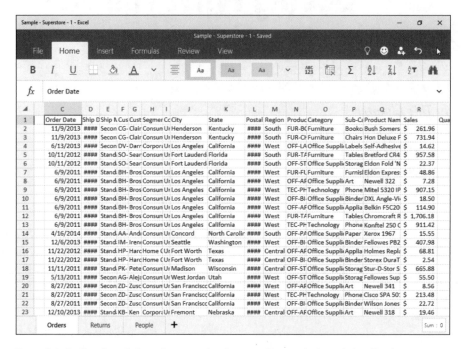

Figure 2-1: An Excel worksheet that contains data needing analysis and visualization.

In the following sections, we use Tableau to analyze and visualize the data contained within this same Excel worksheet.

Connecting to your data in Tableau

Tableau can use many different types of data sources, ranging from text and Excel to all the best databases in the world. In Chapter 4, we discuss data sources in more detail, but for this example, we use the sample Excel worksheet shown in Figure 2-1. (This sample worksheet is included in the standard installation of Tableau, so you may want to use it to follow along with the example.)

To begin analyzing data, you need to open Tableau and then connect to the data file. To do so, follow these steps:

1. **Click the Tableau icon on your desktop (or your Start menu) to open the application.**

   Doing so displays the Tableau Start page, as shown in Figure 2-2 (you may see different options available).

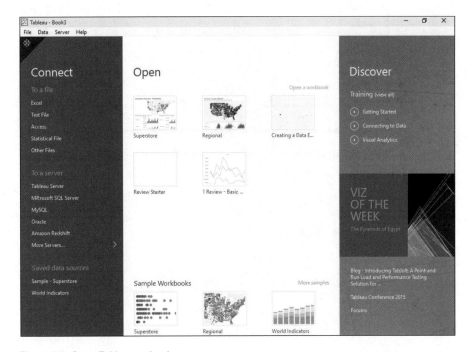

Figure 2-2: Open Tableau to begin.

2. **In the Connect pane at the left side of the Start page, click the Excel link under the To a File heading to display the Open dialog box, as shown in Figure 2-3.**

3. **Using the Open dialog box, select the Excel worksheet that you want to open, and then click the Open button to continue.**

   In this case, choose the Sample-Superstore worksheet. You may need to navigate to the My Tableau Repository folder in the Datasources directory to find it.

   Doing so displays the data source screen shown in Figure 2-4.

Figure 2-3: Use the Open dialog box to locate the Excel worksheet.

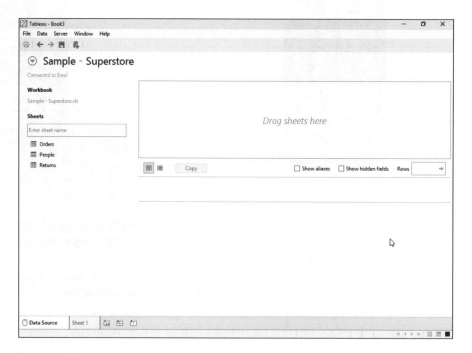

Figure 2-4: The data source screen enables you to choose the sheet that contains the data you want to use.

4. **Select the Orders sheet from the navigation menu on the left and drag it onto the Drag Sheets Here area, as shown in Figure 2-4.**

   For this example, we're done with defining our connection and ready to click the Sheet 1 tab in the lower-left corner of the screen. (Note that a pop-up appears, telling you that you are about to go to the Tableau worksheet associated with the data; refer to Figure 2-5.). This will move you from the Data Source page to the workspace shown in Figure 2-6.

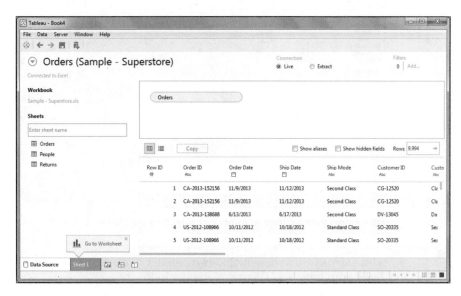

Figure 2-5: Drag the sheet into the box so that you can use the data in your analysis.

Understanding Tableau worksheets

Tableau has three different types of pages that you can use to create and present your data analysis results. These include *worksheets, dashboards,* and *stories.* You'll discover more about each of these page types in later chapters, but for now you need to know the following:

- You use worksheets to create visualizations.

- You use dashboards to combine two or more worksheets that you want to share.

- You use stories as a means of stepping people through worksheets and dashboards with commentary to guide them through your analysis.

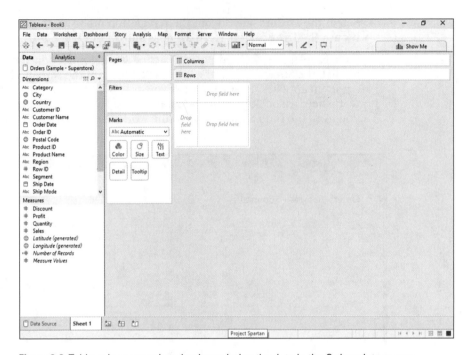

Figure 2-6: Tableau is now ready to begin analyzing the data in the Orders data source.

The Tableau worksheet includes a number of elements that you'll use as you build your analysis. These include the following:

- **Data pane:** This is the area that appears along the left side of the worksheet (in the Side bar) and contains two sections: one labeled Dimensions and one labeled Measures. These sections hold the fields that you can add to the work area to perform the analysis. The Side bar also has a tab labeled Analytics that's used to add things like trend lines to a visualization.

- **Shelves and cards:** These are the areas in the workspace with names like Pages, Filters, Marks, and so on where you drag fields from the Data pane to produce a visualization. Your visualization will change depending on where you drop a field, so later chapters will provide much more detailed information about using shelves and cards.

- **New Worksheet, New Dashboard, and New Story buttons:** These buttons enable you to add new pages to your visualization.

- **Menu bar:** Here you'll find various commands for working with Tableau such as File, Data, and Format.

- **Toolbar:** This bar contains a number of buttons that enable you to perform various tasks with a click, such as Save, Undo, and New Worksheet.

✔ **Show Me:** Clicking this label displays a palette that gives you quick access to different options that are appropriate for visualizing the selected types of fields. The palette changes depending on which fields you have selected or are active in the worksheet.

Hovering over different options in Show Me will tell you what fields are needed to bring those chart types to life.

Starting to analyze data

Almost everyone is used to seeing bar charts that graphically display results comparing data for different products, different sub-categories, and so on. For a first example, we'll create a bar chart in Tableau so that you can see just how easy it is to do.

To create a bar chart that analyzes sales by sub-category, follow these steps:

1. **In the sample workbook created earlier in this chapter, drag the Sales field from the Measures section of the Data pane and drop it onto the Columns shelf to produce the result shown in Figure 2-7.**

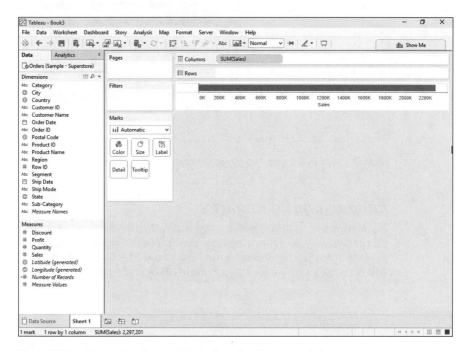

Figure 2-7: Begin creating the analysis by dropping Sales onto Columns.

> 2. **Next, drag Sub-category from the Dimensions section of the Data pane and drop it onto the Rows shelf, as shown in Figure 2-8.**

So, with just two steps, you've created a simple bar chart that provides an analysis of sales broken down by sub-category. The task doesn't get much simpler than that!

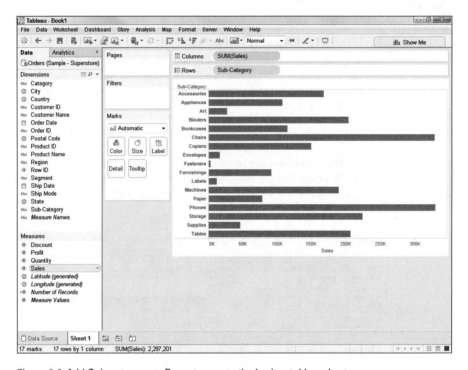

Figure 2-8: Add Sub-category to Rows to create the horizontal bar chart.

Enhancing the analysis

Now, suppose that you'd like to go a step further and make the analysis even more useful by also showing how profitable the sales were. Tableau provides several options, depending upon how you'd like to display the results. We will now take a quick look at a couple of these methods to see what happens.

Adding a secondary bar chart

One of the fields that's available in the Data pane is Profit, so we can use that field in a number of different ways to enhance Tableau's analysis. If you'd like to show profit as a secondary bar chart, simply drag and drop Profit onto the Columns shelf to the right of where you dropped Sales. Figure 2-9 displays the result.

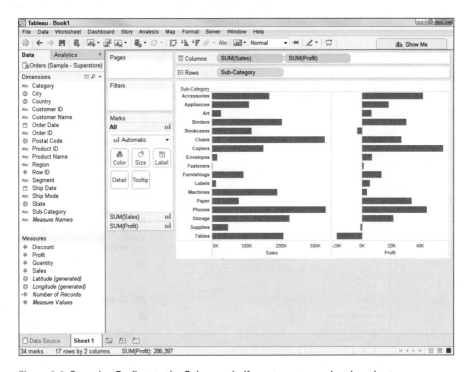

Figure 2-9: Dropping Profit onto the Columns shelf creates a secondary bar chart.

Adding a new bar to the original chart

Although the secondary bar chart does display the profits for each sub-category, you might not find that this type of chart is particularly intuitive. A better option might be to add a second bar to the original chart so that viewers can see a bit more clearly how sales and profits are linked in each sub-category.

To modify the chart, do the following:

1. **Click the Undo button (the left-pointing arrow on the toolbar) to revert to the way the chart appeared before Profit was dropped on the Columns shelf.**

2. **Drag Profit and drop it on the Sales axis at the bottom of the chart.**

   As Figure 2-10 shows, the chart now displays bars for both profit and sales on the same chart.

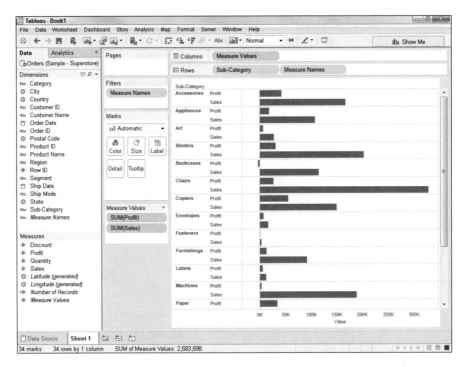

Figure 2-10: Dropping Profit onto the Sales axis creates a combined bar chart.

Using color to depict profitability

Now, suppose that rather than having separate bars for profit and sales, you'd like to use different colors to indicate how profitable your sales were in each of the sub-categories. Once again, Tableau makes this an easy task.

To make this change to the chart, again click the Undo button to remove the bar for profit from the chart. Next, click Profit and drag it to Color on the Marks card. Now Tableau shows the profitability of sales in each sub-category on a continuous color scale, as shown in Figure 2-11.

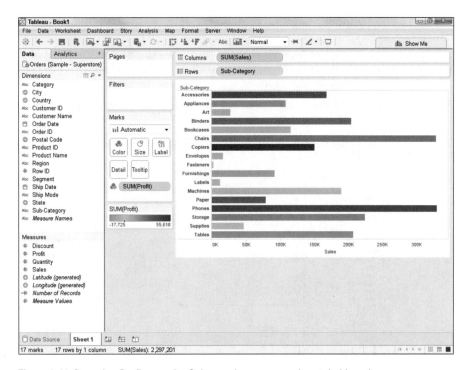

Figure 2-11: Dropping Profit onto the Color card creates a color-coded bar chart.

Displaying results on a map

Finally, how about creating another chart that shows sales values geographically? In this case, we'll display state sales on a map with different-sized symbols to indicate each state's sales.

You're going to want to put the Sales-by-State map on a separate sheet rather than modifying the existing bar chart. Doing so will enable you to later show both charts on a Tableau dashboard.

TIP

You'll want to give your sheets descriptive names. This makes it easier when you're ready to build a dashboard, because you don't have to look at what's on each sheet to decide which ones to use. You can rename a sheet by double-clicking the sheet name (which appears below the workspace) and then typing whatever name you want to use.

To create the Sales-by-State map, follow these steps:

1. **Click the New Worksheet button — the one to the right of the worksheet name tab near the bottom of the workspace — to create a new sheet for the map.**

2. **Hold down the Control key while you select the fields State and Sales in the Data pane.**

3. **Click the Show Me button to display the Chart palette, as shown in Figure 2-12.**

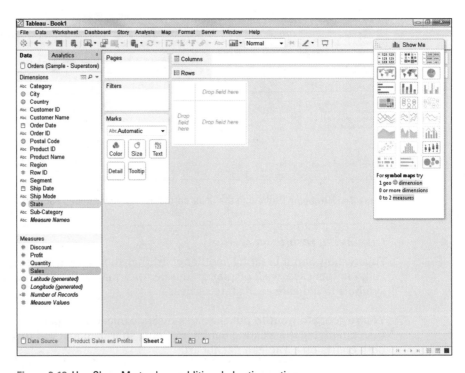

Figure 2-12: Use Show Me to show additional charting options.

4. **Click the Symbol Maps option — the first option in the second row from the top — to display the data using differently sized symbols to represent sales for each state.**

5. **Click the Show Me button again to hide the Chart palette and display your State Sales map, as shown in Figure 2-13.**

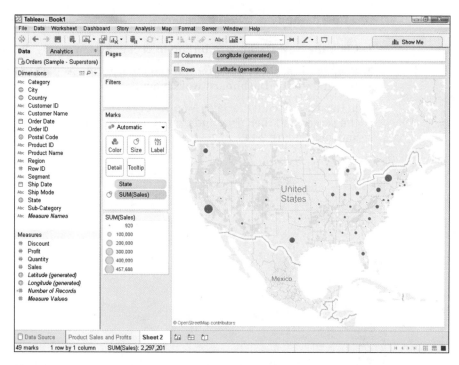

Figure 2-13: Tableau displays the sales map.

You'll probably want to rename this worksheet to something like Sales Map. As mentioned previously, renaming worksheets is pretty easy — just double-click the current sheet name and then type whatever name you want to use.

You can create additional sheets containing further analytic findings, but for now, we'll move on to using the sheets we have to make a dashboard.

Creating Dashboards

In Tableau, you perform ad hoc analysis and create visualizations on each worksheet, but you'll often want to use a Tableau dashboard to bring together your visualizations and create interactive applications for your audience. In this section, you'll see how to create a clear and effective dashboard.

To create a dashboard, follow these steps:

1. **Click the New Dashboard button to create a new, empty dashboard.**

2. **Drag the first sheet that you want to incorporate as part of the dashboard onto the Dashboard workspace.**

   In this case, locate the Sales Map Sheet tab in the lower-left corner of the screen and then drag and drop it onto the Dashboard workspace, as shown in Figure 2-14.

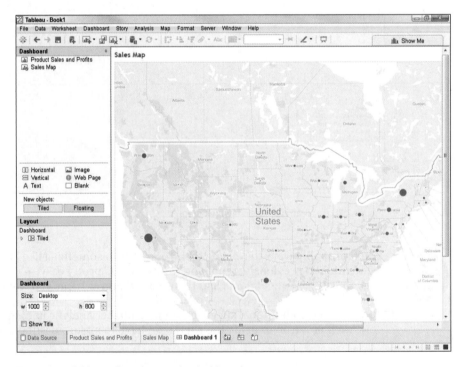

Figure 2-14: Add your first sheet to the dashboard.

3. **Drag the second sheet that you want to use onto the Dashboard workspace.**

   It doesn't matter in what order you created the sheets; you can add them as needed to the dashboard.

   This time, you'll want to drop the Sales vs. Profits Sheet tab onto the Dashboard workspace.

   As Figure 2-15 shows, Tableau indicates where the second chart will appear on the workspace by displaying a dark gray rectangle.

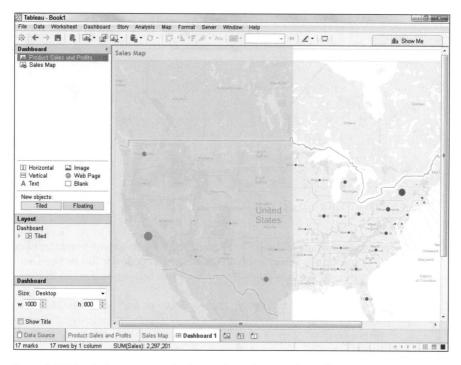

Figure 2-15: The dark gray rectangle shows where the new chart will appear on the dashboard.

4. **Release the mouse button to drop the chart in the indicated location, as shown in Figure 2-16.**

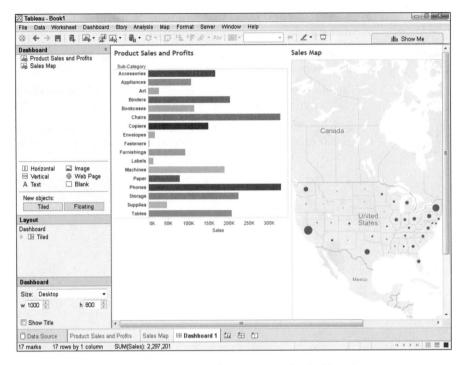

Figure 2-16: Drop the chart where you want it to appear on the dashboard.

5. **(Optional) If desired, change the target size of your dashboard by making a selection from the Size drop-down list in the Dashboard section of the navigation menu on the left, as shown in Figure 2-17.**

As you'll find out in later chapters, you can add additional sheets, titles, and so on to a dashboard to further enhance your visualization. You can also add filters so that viewers can choose to see only the information that matters to them.

If sheets don't seem to fit properly onto your dashboard, click the sheet on the dashboard and then select the appropriate Fit option from the toolbar.

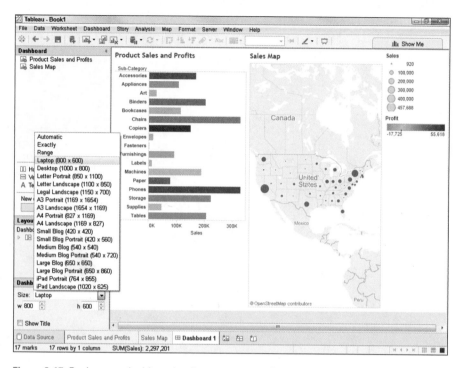

Figure 2-17: Resize your dashboard to fit your target audience.

Telling the Story

Sometimes you'll want to share a specific insight with your audience, and you'll want to help the audience understand the process that you went through to get there. Tableau makes it possible for you to do so using stories. A *story* is a special type of Tableau sheet that contains worksheets or dashboards connected in sequence as *story points*.

When you create a story in Tableau, you add the worksheets and dashboards in the sequence that you want them to appear in the story. The story points appear as blocks of text above the worksheets and dashboards. You can use them to explain your analysis to viewers, who can click to find out what's next.

Effectively, using Tableau Story Points allows you to provide an interactive narrative to your visualizations so people can follow your path to insight. Chapter 11 provides additional information on Tableau stories.

3

Understanding the Basics

In This Chapter

▶ Getting started with Tableau Desktop

▶ Making the data connection

▶ Understanding dimensions and measures

▶ Selecting the right type of chart

▶ Changing the view

*T*ableau is almost certainly very different from any software application that you've used in the past. With its highly visual approach to data analysis, Tableau can seem a little intimidating when you're just getting started. This chapter provides you with a more comprehensive look at the basics you need to understand to really feel comfortable working with the software on your own.

Getting to Know the Tableau Desktop Environment

Getting to know Tableau Desktop means getting to know several different pages and workspaces. What you see in Tableau will depend on what you are trying to accomplish. Rather than presenting a cluttered workspace overloaded with controls and dialogue boxes, Tableau provides visual cues to suit the task at hand. Now we take a deeper look at what you can expect to see.

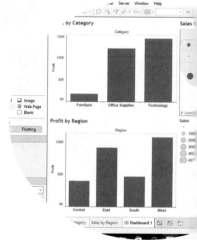

Looking at the Tableau Start page

Tableau works with all kinds of source data that can be located almost anywhere as long as it's accessible to the user. That source could be an Excel file, a text file, or a database. To do anything in Tableau, then, you first have to specify your data source or sources. That's why, when you first start Tableau, you see the Start page shown in Figure 3-1.

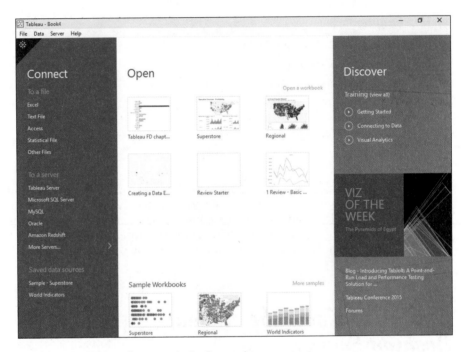

Figure 3-1: The Tableau Start page is the first workspace you see.

Tableau works using your existing data, so you must have access to some type of source data first.

The Tableau Start page was briefly discussed in Chapter 1, but as a quick reminder, the page contains three distinct sections:

- **Connect:** You use this section when you want to start a new data connection in your Tableau workbook. Tableau Desktop has two editions, and the type of edition you're using will change the options you have to choose from. Tableau Desktop Personal Edition is for connections to file-based data sources like Excel and Microsoft Access, and also includes several cloud-based data sources. Tableau Desktop Professional Edition allows you to go beyond the files and additionally connect to databases hosted on servers. More information on these differences and data connection options can be found in Chapter 4.

✔ **Open:** You use this section to open and continue working on an existing Tableau workbook. The existing workbook can be one that you've created or one of the samples that Tableau Software provides for training purposes.

✔ **Discover:** This section gives you easy access to training resources as well as news about Tableau.

When you make a selection on the Tableau Start page, you'll need to use the Open dialog box that appears to navigate your computer's file system so that you can locate the data source or workbook you want to open.

Understanding the Data Source Page

Depending upon your data source, you'll probably see the Data Source Page similar to Figure 3-2 after you connect to the data source. The reason you'll see this workspace is that typical data sources usually contain more than one set of related data. In the case of an actual database file, each set would be one of the tables in the database. In the case of an Excel workbook, you might have related data appearing on separate sheets.

See Chapters 4 and 5 for more information on data connections.

In Figure 3-2, the three sheets of an Excel workbook each contain data that can be used for data analysis in Tableau, and two of the sheets (Orders and Returns) were dragged into the window near the upper right of the workspace. In this case, Tableau recognized common fields between the two tables and automatically suggested a join, as shown on the diagram shown in the picture. Note that if you need to change how Tableau combines the data you can right-click the join and choose your preferred option.

You can use the Live and Extract options under the Connection heading to control whether Tableau automatically updates your data analysis when the source data changes. The default Live connection enables Tableau to see any new or changed data. You can use the Extract option when you need to base your analysis on a snapshot in time. You may also want to use the Extract option if you're dealing with a very slow data connection and would rather update your data as needed after you've finished building your analysis.

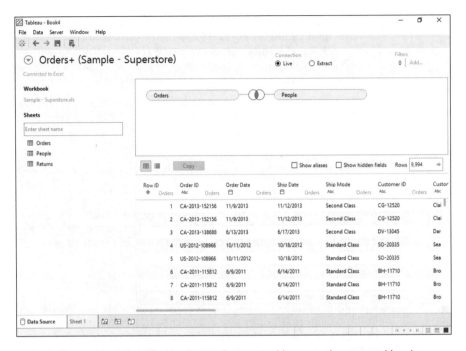

Figure 3-2: The Tableau Data Connection workspace enables you to how to combine data.

If you don't need to base your analysis on the entire data set, you can add a *filter* to the extract so that Tableau can use the specified subset of the data (which may also improve performance).

Using worksheets to explore data

Worksheets are where you'll be spending most of your time in Tableau. As you can see in Figure 3-3, this is the place where you create the visualizations that you'll use in dashboards and stories.

As you drag and drop items from the Data pane running down the left side of the screen onto the shelves and cards in the workspace, you'll see immediate results displayed graphically. This interactive display means that you can easily experiment and simply click the toolbar's Undo button if you aren't satisfied with the results.

If you take a close look at the fields that appear in the Data pane, you'll notice that each of them has an icon to the left of the field name that indicates the type of data that's contained in the field. For example, in Figure 3-3, you can see Text fields, Geographical Location fields, Date fields, and Numeric fields. The type of field you use in your view will affect how Tableau determines the recommended display. For example, geographic fields can be seen on a map while date fields usually are shown as line charts.

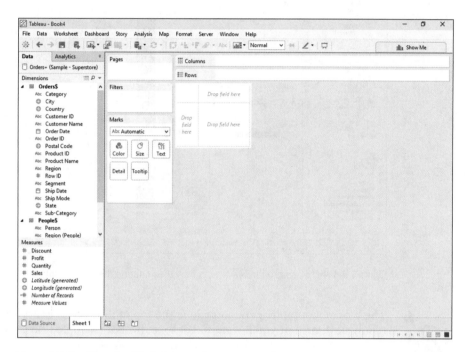

Figure 3-3: You'll use the Worksheet workspace most often.

Dragging and dropping fields onto either the Columns or Rows shelf controls the edges of the chart, helping to define the structure of the view. Dragging and dropping fields onto the Marks card controls the display of the marks within the view. For example, if you drag Profit onto the Rows shelf and Category onto the Columns shelf, the chart will display a vertical bar chart with the height of the bars representing the relative profit for each category. The Profit measure creates an axis on one edge of our view, and Category creates labels on the other. If you then drag Profit from Measures onto the Color card, the bars will no longer be the same color, but instead will have colors representing each category's profits on a sliding scale, as shown in Figure 3-4.

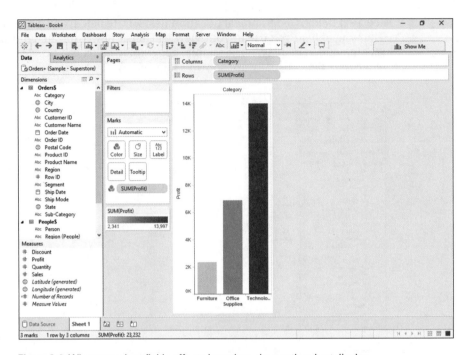

Figure 3-4: Where you drop fields affects how they change the chart display.

The Worksheet toolbar running along the top of the screen contains several handy buttons that you'll want to get to know. For example, the Duplicate Worksheet button gives you a quick way to create a copy of the current worksheet that you can easily modify as needed without affecting the current worksheet. Hover your mouse pointer over a button briefly to display a tooltip with the name of the button.

Getting to know the Dashboard workspace

Although you can certainly share your Tableau worksheets, in most cases, you'll probably want to take your worksheets and create dashboards from them so that viewers can get the big picture. Each worksheet essentially contains a single visualization (although you can have multiple items such as sales and profits compared on that visualization). Bringing different worksheets onto a dashboard allows viewers to see multiple visualizations at once in a more comprehensive presentation of the analyses.

See Chapter 10 for more information on dashboards.

Figure 3-5 shows a Tableau dashboard that combines three worksheets to provide a visualization of profit and sales. You can, of course, include additional elements on a dashboard as needed.

Figure 3-5: Use dashboards to present more comprehensive analyses in one place.

 Worksheets and dashboards are linked interactively. This means that changes you make on one of them are reflected on the other. For example, if you change the type of visualization used within a worksheet, any dashboard using that worksheet will also be updated. The top section of the Dashboard panel is called the Dashboard window and lists all the worksheets that currently exist in your workbook. To add a worksheet to the dashboard, simply drag and drop it onto the Dashboard workspace where you want it to appear.

 If you're not able to drop objects in the precise layout you'd like, try clicking the Floating button in the Dashboard panel on the left instead of the Tiled button. That way, Tableau won't try to force you to place objects into a grid layout.

You aren't limited to just adding worksheets to your dashboard. You can add text, images, or even web pages using the buttons that appear below the list of your worksheets in the Dashboard window. One example of how you might find this useful would be to add an image containing your company logo to brand your dashboard and identify with your internal audience.

You'll also find the size options near the bottom of the Dashboard panel quite useful. You can choose options that are appropriate for various screen sizes or even ones that ensure that your dashboard can easily be displayed in a blog posting.

If you select the Show Title check box in the Size section of the Dashboard panel, the dashboard name will appear at the top of the dashboard. If you use this option, you'll almost certainly want to give the dashboard a descriptive name that better tells viewers what the dashboard is all about.

Understanding the Story workspace

At times, the most effective way to get your point across is to tell a story step by step. The Tableau Story workspace, as shown in Figure 3-6, provides you with the means to develop your story.

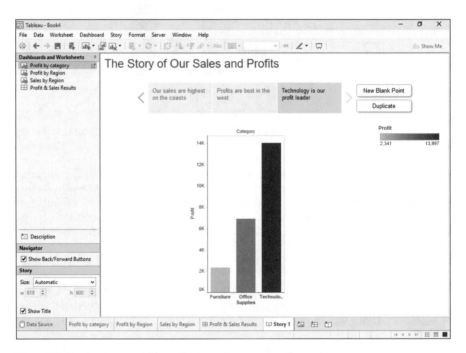

Figure 3-6: Use stories to guide people through your analysis step by step.

You can use both worksheets and dashboards in a Tableau story. You add these elements to the lower area of the Story workspace by dragging and dropping. The gray boxes that appear near the top of the workspace are called *story points,* and you use them to explain each step of the story.

After you've created a story point and added whatever elements you want to appear in that step, you click the New Blank Point button or the Duplicate button to add the next step in your story. (Refer to Figure 3-6.) The difference between the two buttons is whether you want to include the same elements in the next step. In some cases, you may want to build upon your story by adding a visualization that complements what's already there.

See Chapter 11 for more about stories.

Connecting to Your Data

As mentioned earlier in this chapter, Tableau uses data from external files and databases. In most cases, Tableau uses a live connection so that any changes or updates in the source data are reflected in your analyses and visualizations.

Tableau Personal Edition is designed to connect to relatively simple data sources. If you need to use data from a database server more sophisticated than Microsoft Access, you'll need a license for Tableau Professional Edition.

In the world of *relational* databases, you can combine tables using *joins.* Several types of joins exist, including inner, left, right, and full outer joins. These refer to how the database handles records that exist in one table and not in another. Different databases offer varying support for join types, so you may notice that the join options available within Tableau may vary depending on which connection type you use.

Editing your data source

If you've created a Tableau workbook using a data source that changes in location, you might have issues with the visualizations in your workbook. Fortunately, Tableau provides you with the option of editing your data sources if this type of situation arises.

To edit your data source, follow these steps:

1. **Select your existing data source from the Data menu and then select Edit Data Source from the submenu that appears, as shown in Figure 3-7.**

   Note that, for this example, we're assuming the location of our Excel file has moved.

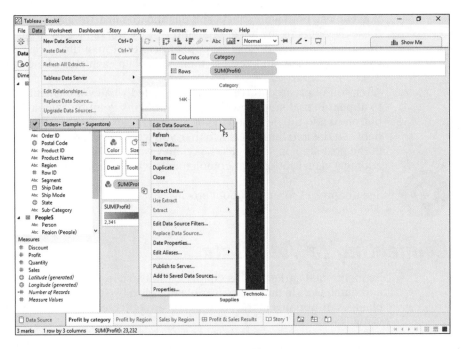

Figure 3-7: Use the Edit Data Source command to modify your existing data source.

2. **Choose Data ⇨ Edit Connection from the main menu, as shown in Figure 3-8, to display the Open dialog box.**

3. **Using the Open dialog box, navigate to the location of your new data source and select the source that you want to use, as shown in Figure 3-9.**

4. **Click the Open button to continue.**

   Tableau connects to the new data source and returns you to the Data Source Page so that you can make any necessary adjustments.

After you've created views and dashboards based off of a data source, you can use them for a different data source without having to build everything all over again. Creating a copy of the workbook and then editing the data source in the copy allows you to keep the views but have them updated with new data. As long as the field names are the same or similar, the transition is quick and easy.

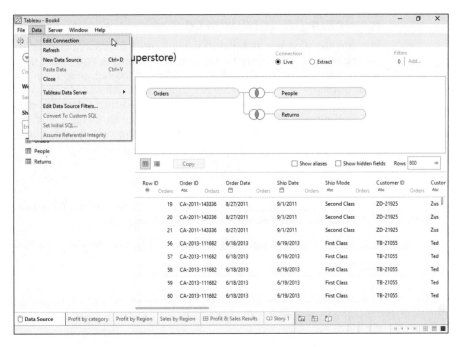

Figure 3-8: Select Data ⇨ Edit Connection.

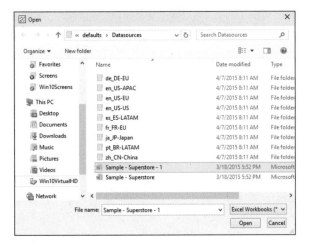

Figure 3-9: Choose your new data source.

Replacing a data source

In some cases, you may need to make a more extensive change to the data source used by a Tableau workbook. For example, you might use a local data source in creating your workbook, but need to change to a data source that's been published to Tableau Server to make it easier to share your analyses and visualizations. The previous method of editing a data source allows you to edit the connection but requires it be of the same type, such as Excel to Excel. Replacing the data source, however, can switch your connection from Excel to SQL Server or any other Tableau connection option.

To replace a data source, follow these steps:

1. **In the Data Connection workspace, choose Data ➪ New Data Source from the main menu, as shown in Figure 3-10.**

2. **In the Connect panel (see Figure 3-11), choose the type of data source you want to use.**

   Doing so brings up the Open dialog box.

3. **Using the Open dialog box, navigate to the data source that you want to use and click the Open button to continue, as shown in Figure 3-12.**

4. **Click a worksheet tab to open a new worksheet.**

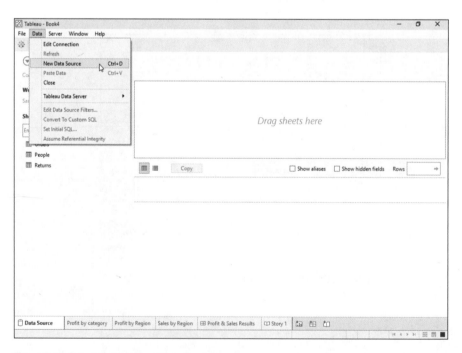

Figure 3-10: Select Data ➪ New Data Source.

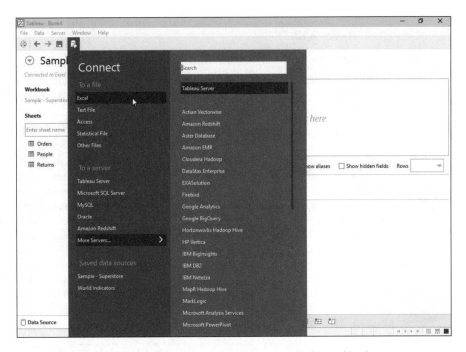

Figure 3-11: Choose the type of data source you want to use in the workbook.

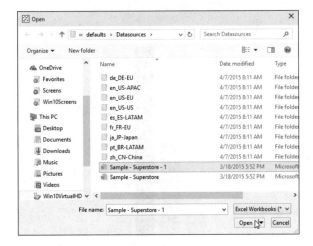

Figure 3-12: Choose the new data source.

5. **Choose Data ⇨ Replace Data Source from the main menu, as shown in Figure 3-13.**

   The Replace Data Source dialog box appears.

6. **Using the dialog box's drop-down menus, choose your current and replacement data sources, as shown in Figure 3-14, and then click OK.**

   Your data source is updated.

If the new data source is slightly different from the original, Tableau will still be able to switch to the new connection. Any fields that have changed in name or data type will provide errors in the Data pane, seen as red exclamation marks. By right-clicking on the field with the error, an option to replace the field references helps you to update the field from the original data connection with the appropriate field from the new connection. This is true for both replacing and editing the data source.

This is what it looks like if you are switching from one data file to another. The dialog boxes will look slightly different if you are switching to a database on a server, but the concepts are the same.

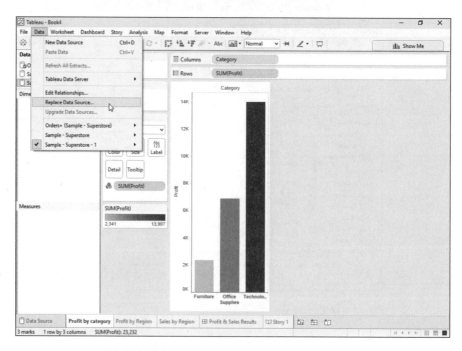

Figure 3-13: Select Data ⇨ Replace Data Source.

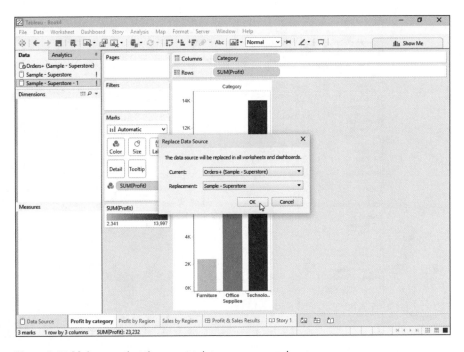

Figure 3-14: Make sure that the correct data sources are shown.

Working with Dimensions and Measures

You've probably noticed that Tableau separates data fields into *dimensions* and *measures,* as shown in Figure 3-15. (Check out the headings in the Data pane on the left in the figure.) It's useful to understand how Tableau decides what fields to place in each area.

Understanding dimensions

Tableau treats any field that contains qualitative, categorical information such as text or dates as dimensions. These types of fields typically produce labels when you add them to the Rows or Columns shelves in a view.

Dimensions enable you to provide detail in a view and to effectively slice or categorize your data. For example, you might be interested in seeing aggregated sales values by state or month, both dimensions that provide more detail.

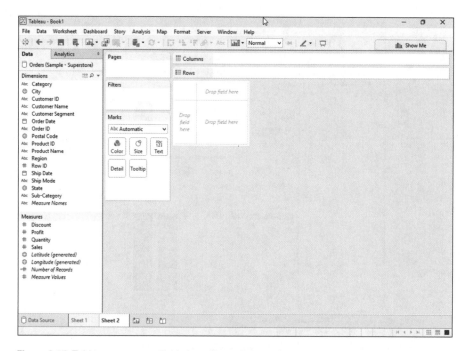

Figure 3-15: Tableau separates fields into dimensions and measures.

Understanding measures

Measures are fields that contain quantitative (or numeric) values that you can do math on (sum, count, and so on). These types of fields typically produce the axes on a chart and are the numbers we use to evaluate whether results are good or bad.

TIP

As a rule of thumb, most measures are numbers and most dimensions are non-numeric. Think about it in these terms. If you do math on it, it is probably a measure. If you use it to slice the data, it is a dimension. However, in some cases, a number may be a dimension. For example, while an order id may be a number, would you ever add up your order #'s or take an average of order #? You may, however, look at the Total Sales amount by order, so using the order id as a dimension would be preferred.

Choosing Chart Types

If you've done a bit of data analysis, you no doubt realize that different
types of questions are best visualized using different types of charts. Simple
bar charts may be familiar, but they don't suit every analytical need and
could lack in visual impact. For example, imagine if you wanted to show
sales results broken down by state. A typical bar chart like the one shown
in Figure 3-16 arranges the states in alphabetical order, but it's a bit hard to
visualize how the results compare geographically.

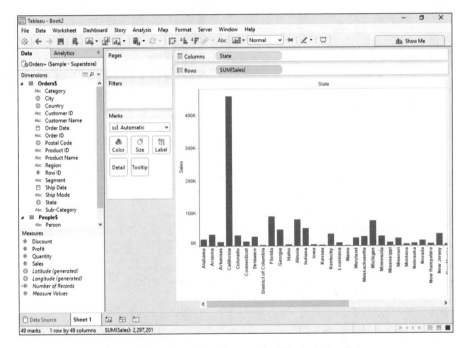

Figure 3-16: A typical bar chart arranged with states in alphabetical order.

Tableau can also sort the chart so that the states appear sorted by sales, as
shown in Figure 3-17, but it's still hard to actually visualize how these results
compare geographically.

To make the results easier to visualize geographically, you might want to try
the Symbol map, as shown in Figure 3-18. With sales depicted as differently
sized circles, it's easy to see where most of the company's sales are happening.

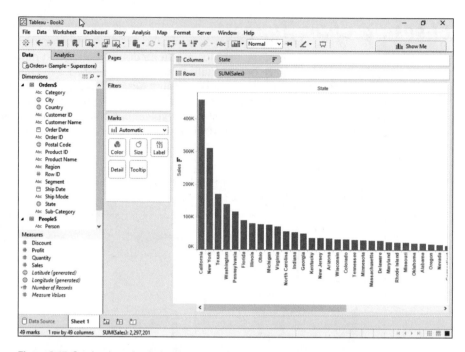

Figure 3-17: Sorting by sales helps, but the results are still difficult to visualize.

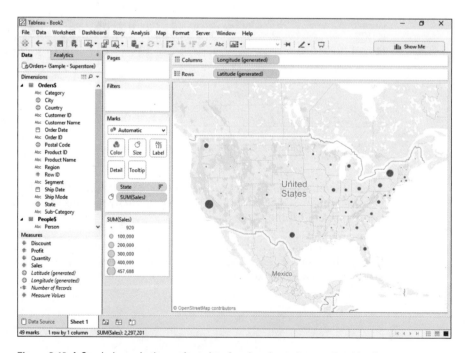

Figure 3-18: A Symbol map is the perfect view for showing sales geographically.

Choosing the best type of chart to visualize your analysis is often a matter of trial and error. Fortunately, the Tableau Show Me palette (see Figure 3-19) makes trying different options easy because all you need to do is point and click. (Note that not all chart options are shown on the Show Me palette; Tableau has far more options available.)

Figure 3-19: Popular chart types displayed in the Show Me palette.

Show Me includes some popular chart types, and it lets you know which ones you can use by graying out types that don't fit the current data in the view or selected in the Data pane.

TIP

While Show Me gives you lots of great ideas, it is also helpful to understand some basics of visual best practices. Search the web for "Tableau Visual Analysis Best Practices: A Guidebook" and you can download a white-paper with lots of great additional information to help you chose the best chart type.

Modifying Your View

Tableau gives you a number of different tools to help you modify the view of the visualization. We take a quick look at a couple of them here.

Figure 3-20 points out several useful tools:

- ✐ **Transpose:** This button swaps the position of the items on the Columns and Rows shelves. By clicking this button, you can quickly switch between horizontal and vertical bar charts, for example.

- ✐ **Sort Descending:** This button sorts a Dimension list in descending order.

- ✐ **Sort Ascending:** This button sorts a Dimension list in ascending order.

- ✐ **Show Me:** This displays the Show Me palette so that you can quickly choose different chart types.

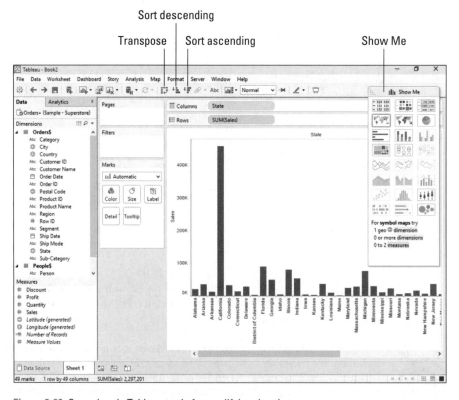

Figure 3-20: Some handy Tableau tools for modifying the view.

If your visualization doesn't fit properly on the screen, click the View List box on the toolbar and select Fit Width, Fit Height, or Entire View instead of the default Normal option. Depending on your chart, you might have to experiment and see which one works best. For example, in Figure 3-19, trying to view the entire chart on a small screen without scrolling will probably make the state names unreadable.

Part II
Bringing in Data

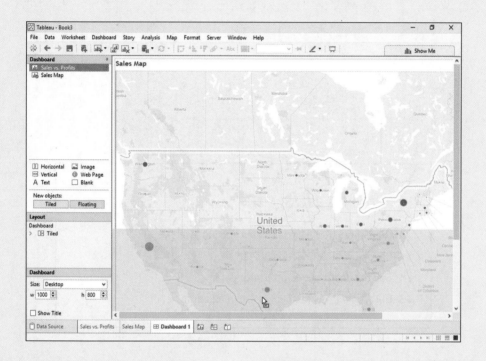

Explore more about data sources and Tableau at www.dummies.com/extras/
tableau.

In this part . . .

✔ Work through the kinds of data you can use.

✔ Choose your connection types.

✔ See the best ways to prep your data.

✔ Get a handle on Tableau shelves and cards.

4

Understanding Data Connections

In This Chapter

▶ Connecting to your data

▶ Understanding the kinds of data you can use

▶ Choosing the type of connection

*T*ableau is a very powerful tool, but without a usable source data, it's a tool looking for work. If you don't have the data you need, you can't do any analyses or visualizations. This chapter takes a deeper dive into what Tableau considers usable data sources and how you can choose to import that data.

Understanding Data Sources

Modern companies live on data. They gather data on everything from inventory costs to labor costs to the smallest details involving sales. All this raw data can then be transformed, aggregated, and analyzed into submission to create useful business information that can help drive competitive decision making.

But before any of the data can be analyzed, it needs to be stored in an accessible and useful form. Now we take a look at what this means.

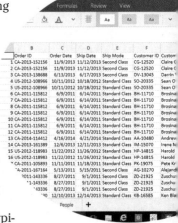

Considering how data is stored

To actually use or analyze data, the data needs to be stored in a standardized format. In the days before computers, this typically meant writing everything down in a ledger. The ledger contained a number of columns that were used for specific purposes, such as the date of the transaction, the type of transaction, the amount of money involved, names of the people involved, and other various details. All of this information was written in by hand, but the bookkeepers always followed the same format so that the information could be more easily understood.

When computers came along, it quickly became clear that the old handwritten ledger could be replaced by a computerized database. What was also clear is the fact that the database needed to have a formal structure similar to that of the old-time ledger, because this formal structure made it possible for the computer to process the data.

Figure 4-1 shows an example of the type of structure that evolved. Different types of data are stored in individual fields (columns) and all the information about a specific transaction is stored in a record (row).

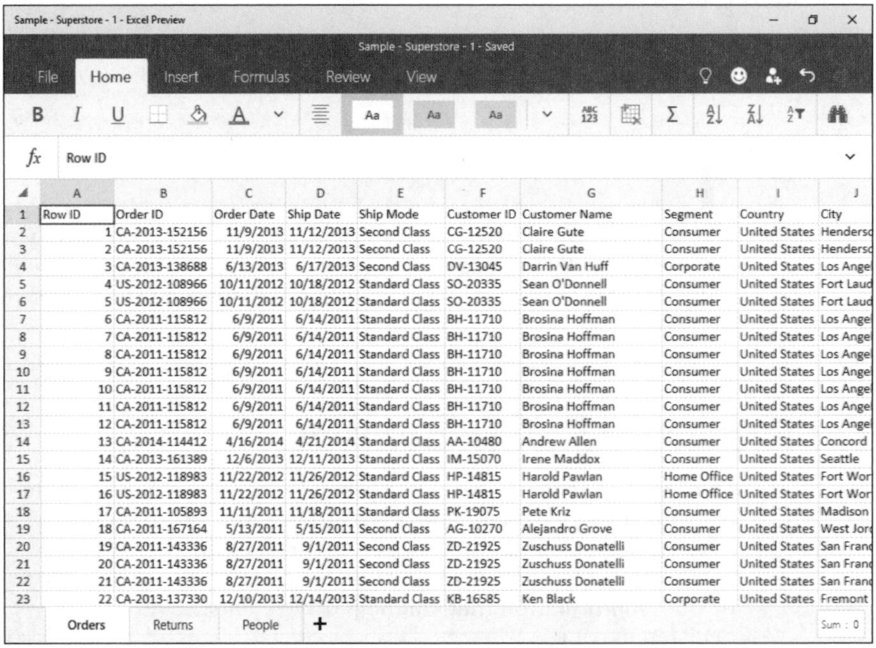

	A	B	C	D	E	F	G	H	I	J
1	Row ID	Order ID	Order Date	Ship Date	Ship Mode	Customer ID	Customer Name	Segment	Country	City
2	1	CA-2013-152156	11/9/2013	11/12/2013	Second Class	CG-12520	Claire Gute	Consumer	United States	Henders
3	2	CA-2013-152156	11/9/2013	11/12/2013	Second Class	CG-12520	Claire Gute	Consumer	United States	Henders
4	3	CA-2013-138688	6/13/2013	6/17/2013	Second Class	DV-13045	Darrin Van Huff	Corporate	United States	Los Ange
5	4	US-2012-108966	10/11/2012	10/18/2012	Standard Class	SO-20335	Sean O'Donnell	Consumer	United States	Fort Laud
6	5	US-2012-108966	10/11/2012	10/18/2012	Standard Class	SO-20335	Sean O'Donnell	Consumer	United States	Fort Laud
7	6	CA-2011-115812	6/9/2011	6/14/2011	Standard Class	BH-11710	Brosina Hoffman	Consumer	United States	Los Ange
8	7	CA-2011-115812	6/9/2011	6/14/2011	Standard Class	BH-11710	Brosina Hoffman	Consumer	United States	Los Ange
9	8	CA-2011-115812	6/9/2011	6/14/2011	Standard Class	BH-11710	Brosina Hoffman	Consumer	United States	Los Ange
10	9	CA-2011-115812	6/9/2011	6/14/2011	Standard Class	BH-11710	Brosina Hoffman	Consumer	United States	Los Ange
11	10	CA-2011-115812	6/9/2011	6/14/2011	Standard Class	BH-11710	Brosina Hoffman	Consumer	United States	Los Ange
12	11	CA-2011-115812	6/9/2011	6/14/2011	Standard Class	BH-11710	Brosina Hoffman	Consumer	United States	Los Ange
13	12	CA-2011-115812	6/9/2011	6/14/2011	Standard Class	BH-11710	Brosina Hoffman	Consumer	United States	Los Ange
14	13	CA-2014-114412	4/16/2014	4/21/2014	Standard Class	AA-10480	Andrew Allen	Consumer	United States	Concord
15	14	CA-2013-161389	12/6/2013	12/11/2013	Standard Class	IM-15070	Irene Maddox	Consumer	United States	Seattle
16	15	US-2012-118983	11/22/2012	11/26/2012	Standard Class	HP-14815	Harold Pawlan	Home Office	United States	Fort Wor
17	16	US-2012-118983	11/22/2012	11/26/2012	Standard Class	HP-14815	Harold Pawlan	Home Office	United States	Fort Wor
18	17	CA-2011-105893	11/11/2011	11/18/2011	Standard Class	PK-19075	Pete Kriz	Consumer	United States	Madison
19	18	CA-2011-167164	5/13/2011	5/15/2011	Second Class	AG-10270	Alejandro Grove	Consumer	United States	West Jor
20	19	CA-2011-143336	8/27/2011	9/1/2011	Second Class	ZD-21925	Zuschuss Donatelli	Consumer	United States	San Fran
21	20	CA-2011-143336	8/27/2011	9/1/2011	Second Class	ZD-21925	Zuschuss Donatelli	Consumer	United States	San Fran
22	21	CA-2011-143336	8/27/2011	9/1/2011	Second Class	ZD-21925	Zuschuss Donatelli	Consumer	United States	San Fran
23	22	CA-2013-137330	12/10/2013	12/14/2013	Standard Class	KB-16585	Ken Black	Corporate	United States	Fremont

Figure 4-1: This Excel worksheet illustrates a database table structure.

One very important thing to remember about databases is that they all have a defined structure. For example, the Order Date and Ship Date fields would ideally be defined as Date or Date/Time fields, which mean that the database application will only accept valid dates as entries in those fields. Depending on the database, other fields might be defined as Numeric, Currency, Text, Boolean, and so on. This well-defined structure makes it possible for applications like Tableau to understand precisely how to use the data in each field.

Using file-based data sources

Unfortunately, people sometimes use tools to do jobs that aren't totally appropriate for a given task. There is the old saying, "if all you have is a hammer, everything looks like a nail." Using file-based sources like Excel instead of a database is an easy option for many of us, but needs to be done with care. Tableau will read the first few values of each column in the file and will determine a default data type. However, when connecting to a database, Tableau can pick up the definitions of fields from that database, making it more likely for your fields to be consistent.

One of the reasons that people like to use file-based sources like Excel as a database is because they are so flexible. People don't like to be told that they have to enter a valid date or other specific information that may not readily be at hand. Or, a user might decide that she would like to remove a column or use a different name for an existing column. Either way, if you've created a visualization in Tableau based upon the existing structure (and hoping for valid data), your analysis could mysteriously stop functioning properly. As with any data source, be aware that you need consistency in your structure and keep an eye out for errors.

Understanding Different Editions of Tableau Desktop

Tableau comes in both personal and professional editions to support the needs of different organizations. The two editions differ in the types of data sources they support.

Tableau Personal Edition supports connections to file-based data sources such as text files, Microsoft Access databases and Excel workbooks. Connections to Microsoft Windows Azure Marketplace and OData will also be available. Lastly, Tableau Data Extracts (.tde files) can be used and are great for creating local copies of your data in a compressed format.

Tableau Professional Edition supports all the formats supported by the Personal Edition, plus many native connections to server-hosted data sources. The list is long and ever growing as Tableau evolves, consisting of over 40 options of relational, multi-dimensional, and cloud-based databases and repositories. For a complete list, refer to the Data Source Page in Tableau Desktop Professional or to www.tableau.com/products/techspecs.

Considering Live Data versus Data Extracts

In addition to choosing your data source, you need to decide whether you want to use live or static data. In other words, do you want your analysis and visualizations to be based on the most current data that's available or do you want to use an extract that provides a snapshot of the results based on criteria that you select? You might, for example, want to show the results for a specific, limited time frame such as last year or the previous quarter. If your analysis needs to show what's happening right now, you'd want to use a live data connection that will be reflected in your views.

Figure 4-2 shows Tableau's Data Source page with the Extract option selected for the data connection. (This option enables you to import any data you may have stored as a Tableau data extract). Because no filters have yet been specified, Tableau will use all the information in the current data source, but won't automatically update any data analysis or visualizations when the information in that data source changes.

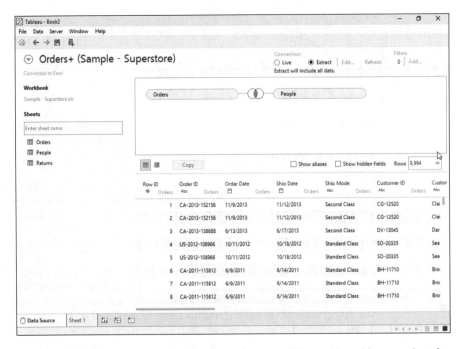

Figure 4-2: Switching from Live to Extract means that you will be working with a snapshot of your data.

There are a number of other reasons that you may chose to use a data extract. The most common one is portability. Let's say that your data resides on a database server like MS SQL Server, but you want to do your analysis while you are on a plane or present your results in a boardroom, where you may not have a live connection to the data. Using a data extract will provide you with the data you need without the hassles of the connection.

If you have Tableau Server, the Extract option can be set to a refresh schedule to be updated when needed.

Suppose, however, that you'd like to limit your analysis and visualizations to a subset of the data contained in the data source. You can do so by applying a filter based on the contents of any field in your data source. For this example, imagine that you want to show what happened in a particular year.

To apply a filter that shows orders only for one year, follow these steps:

1. **In the Data Connection workspace, select the Extract option under the Connection heading.**

2. **Click the Edit link (just to the right of the Extract radio button) to display the Extract Data dialog box, as shown in Figure 4-3.**

Figure 4-3: Use the Extract Data dialog box to limit the amount of data that's used.

3. **In the Extract Data dialog box, click the Add button to display the Add Filter dialog box, as shown in Figure 4-4.**

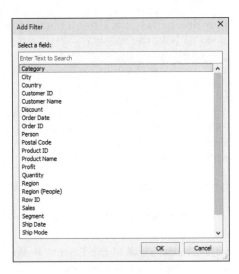

Figure 4-4: Choose the field for filtering.

4. **In the Add Filter dialog box, click the Order Date field and then click the OK button to display the Filter Field [Order Date] dialog box, as shown in Figure 4-5.**

Figure 4-5: Choose the level of filtering.

5. **Because you want to show the orders for a specific year, choose Years and then click Next.**

Doing so brings up the Filter [Year of Order Date] dialog box, as shown in Figure 4-6.

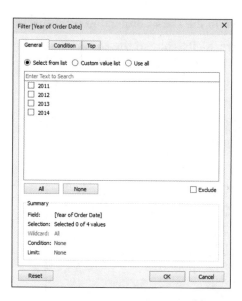

Figure 4-6: Choose the specific condition.

6. **In this case, you want to base your analysis on orders from 2014, so select the 2014 check box and click OK to return to the Extract Data dialog box, as shown in Figure 4-7.**

Figure 4-7: You can now see the details of how the filter would be applied.

7. **Click OK to return to the Data Connection workspace.**

8. **To create the extract, click one of the sheet tabs to display the Save Extract As dialog box, as shown in Figure 4-8.**

You have to save your extract before you can use it.

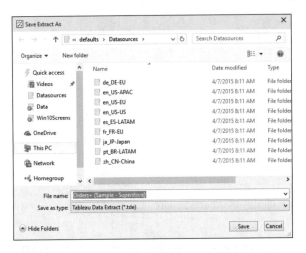

Figure 4-8: You need to save the data extract before you can use it.

9. **Click the Save button to save the data extract.**

After you've saved the data extract, only the filtered data is used in your data analysis and visualizations. In this case, the results will only include data where orders were placed in 2014.

▦ Orders	▦ Orders	▦ Orders	▦ Orders	▦ Orders		▦ Orders	▦ Orders	▦ Orders	▦ Orders	▦ Orders	▦ Ord
▦ People	▦ People	▦ People	▦ People	▦ People		▦ People	▦ People	▦ People	▦ People	▦ People	▦ Peo
▦ Returns	▦ Returns	▦ Returns	▦ Returns	▦ Returns		▦ Returns	▦ Returns	▦ Returns	▦ Returns	▦ Returns	▦ Ret

5

Connecting to Data

In This Chapter

▶ Getting your data ready

▶ Making the connection

▶ Making sure that you're up to date

Tableau is all about helping you analyze and visualize external data. For Tableau to do that for you, you may have to do some prep work. This chapter looks at how you can ensure your data is ready for use in Tableau, how to create a successful connection to the appropriate data set, and how Tableau can help you make sure your data is properly prepared.

Preparing Your Data

Tableau can work with a number of different data sources, depending on the edition of Tableau that you've licensed. (See Chapter 4 for all the details on that point.) Fortunately, true database applications enforce certain rules to ensure that each field in a record contains the proper type of data. For example, users can't enter arbitrary text in numeric or date fields, because this would make it impossible to properly process the information contained in the database.

Tableau works with data where it lives, whether it's in a database, files, or even in the cloud. In this section, we'll discuss working with file-based data sources such as Excel worksheets. Due to the lack of controlled data structure, there are advantages and disadvantages that we'll also address.

Using the data preparation features

Excel worksheets may include extraneous information or have things like blank columns in the middle of the data. Figure 5-1 shows an example of a worksheet with both of these problems.

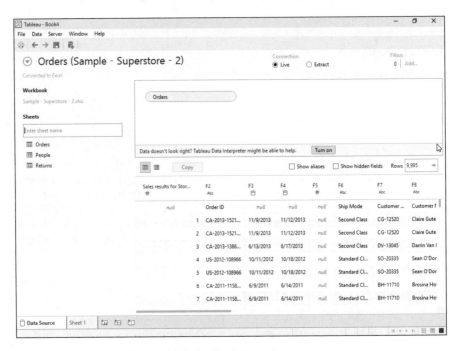

Figure 5-1: This Excel worksheet is missing key information.

Notice that Tableau isn't showing the correct field names. What appear to be the field names are mostly showing up as data in the first row (although several fields display *null* to indicate that the contents are invalid based on the data type of the field). In addition, the field that's labeled F5 appears to be completely filled with invalid data.

The reason that Tableau is having problems with the fields becomes clearer when you take a look at the worksheet back in Excel. (See Figure 5-2.) In this figure, you can see extra rows above the data and a blank column within the data. In addition, the worksheet contains text in cell A1 above the data table.

Sample - Superstore - 2 - Excel Preview

Sample - Superstore - 2 - Saved

	A	B	C	D	E	F	G	H	I	J
1	Sales results for Store 1									
2										
3	Row ID	Order ID	Order Date	Ship Date		Ship Mode	Customer ID	Customer Name	Segment	Country
4	1	CA-2013-152156	11/9/2013	11/12/2013		Second Class	CG-12520	Claire Gute	Consumer	United Stat
5	2	CA-2013-152156	11/9/2013	11/12/2013		Second Class	CG-12520	Claire Gute	Consumer	United Stat
6	3	CA-2013-138688	6/13/2013	6/17/2013		Second Class	DV-13045	Darrin Van Huff	Corporate	United Stat
7	4	US-2012-108966	10/11/2012	10/18/2012		Standard Class	SO-20335	Sean O'Donnell	Consumer	United Stat
8	5	US-2012-108966	10/11/2012	10/18/2012		Standard Class	SO-20335	Sean O'Donnell	Consumer	United Stat
9	6	CA-2011-115812	6/9/2011	6/14/2011		Standard Class	BH-11710	Brosina Hoffman	Consumer	United Stat
10	7	CA-2011-115812	6/9/2011	6/14/2011		Standard Class	BH-11710	Brosina Hoffman	Consumer	United Stat
11	8	CA-2011-115812	6/9/2011	6/14/2011		Standard Class	BH-11710	Brosina Hoffman	Consumer	United Stat
12	9	CA-2011-115812	6/9/2011	6/14/2011		Standard Class	BH-11710	Brosina Hoffman	Consumer	United Stat
13	10	CA-2011-115812	6/9/2011	6/14/2011		Standard Class	BH-11710	Brosina Hoffman	Consumer	United Stat
14	11	CA-2011-115812	6/9/2011	6/14/2011		Standard Class	BH-11710	Brosina Hoffman	Consumer	United Stat
15	12	CA-2011-115812	6/9/2011	6/14/2011		Standard Class	BH-11710	Brosina Hoffman	Consumer	United Stat
16	13	CA-2014-114412	4/16/2014	4/21/2014		Standard Class	AA-10480	Andrew Allen	Consumer	United Stat
17	14	CA-2013-161389	12/6/2013	12/11/2013		Standard Class	IM-15070	Irene Maddox	Consumer	United Stat
18	15	US-2012-118983	11/22/2012	11/26/2012		Standard Class	HP-14815	Harold Pawlan	Home Office	United Stat
19	16	US-2012-118983	11/22/2012	11/26/2012		Standard Class	HP-14815	Harold Pawlan	Home Office	United Stat
20	17	CA-2011-105893	11/11/2011	11/18/2011		Standard Class	PK-19075	Pete Kriz	Consumer	United Stat
21	18	CA-2011-167164	5/13/2011	5/15/2011		Second Class	AG-10270	Alejandro Grove	Consumer	United Stat
22	19	CA-2011-143336	8/27/2011	9/1/2011		Second Class	ZD-21925	Zuschuss Donatelli	Consumer	United Stat
23	20	CA-2011-143336	8/27/2011	9/1/2011		Second Class	ZD-21925	Zuschuss Donatelli	Consumer	United Stat

Orders   Returns   People   +   Sum : 0

Figure 5-2: Looking at the worksheet reveals the problems.

Tableau wants your Excel spreadsheet to look like a database table. What this means is that it expects the first row to contain column headers and each subsequent row to contain data values for each column. It expects the data type in each column to remain consistent and for there to be no extraneous spaces or text inserted anywhere in the spreadsheet. If any of these conditions exist, you will either need to manually clean your spreadsheet or use Tableau's Data Interpreter.

Fortunately, Tableau is pretty good at noticing a problem and will display a prompt asking whether you want its Data Interpreter tool to try to correct any problems that might exist. (Refer to Figure 5-1.) To see whether the Data Interpreter can fix the problems, just click the prompt's Turn On button. Figure 5-3 shows the results of using this tool on the example worksheet.

If you compare Figure 5-1 and Figure 5-3, you see that Tableau now shows the correct field names, no longer has null values in the first record, and has eliminated the empty column from the results.

Always check the data preview area when creating new connections to ensure the data looks as you expect it to.

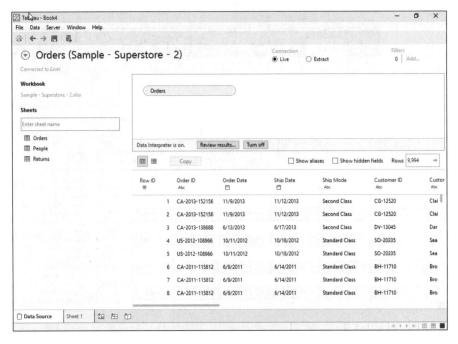

Figure 5-3: The Data Interpreter may be able to fix the problems.

Targeting data sources for manual corrections

Although Tableau can correct many common types of layout and formatting issues automatically, some problems can only be corrected manually. Figure 5-4 demonstrates an example of this type of issue. In this case, the ship dates in records 27 and 28 were not entered correctly, so they show as null rather than as actual dates. If you use this data in Tableau, these null values might give you invalid results.

You may not realize that your data contains null values until you actually start to perform your analysis. In this case, Tableau reports that the table contains a total of 9,994 records, so you may not be concerned about two null values.

Tableau helps us to locate null values, which could also be errors that would need to be corrected in the source data. Although there are only two null values shown above in rows 27 and 28, there could be many more we can't see without scrolling.

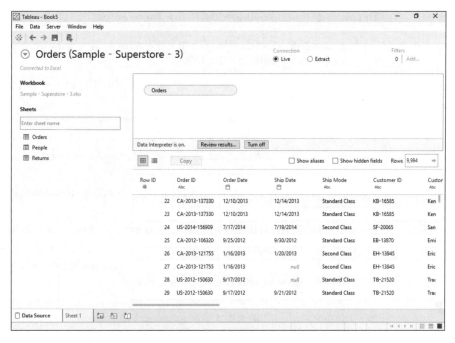

Figure 5-4: The nulls noted are due to empty records in the source data.

Null values just mean that a row contains an empty cell. This does not always mean there is an error in your data. Tableau is well aware of that fact, which is why it gives you options for dealing with null values. Yes, you can use the information Tableau provides to correct entries in the source data, but you can also have Tableau address the values using one of its many functions or remove values with the help of filters.

Establishing a Connection to Your Data Source

Tableau can connect to many different data sources, as referenced in Chapter 4. In this section, we will now look at an example of connecting to Google Analytics, a web service that provides access to website traffic data. This source (like other server data sources) has its own set of security requirements. Generally, however, you'll need to know the connection information for the server you'd like to use as well any required login credentials. Google Analytics is a type of data source that will only require your assigned username and password.

To connect to Google Analytics, follow these steps:

1. **On the Tableau Start page, click the data source type that you want in the Connect panel on the left.**

   You may need to click More Servers to locate the proper server, as shown in Figure 5-5.

2. **In the dialog box that appears, enter your credentials and then sign in by clicking the appropriate button.**

   For Google Analytics, you sign in by entering your Google account name and password, and clicking the Sign In button.

3. **If necessary, perform any extra authentication steps that may be required.**

   For Google Analytics, you click the Accept button to enable Tableau to access your Google Analytics account.

4. **Add the dimensions and measures that you want to use in your analysis, as shown in Figure 5-6.**

   Depending on the type of server that you're connecting to, you may have different steps that you need to complete to finalize your connection.

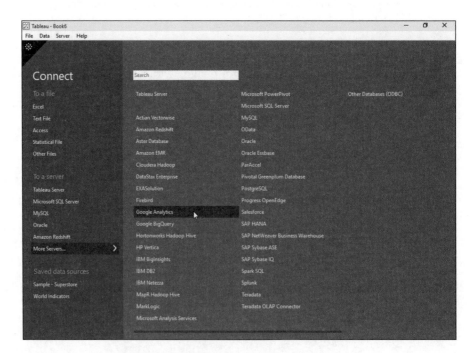

Figure 5-5: Locate and click your server.

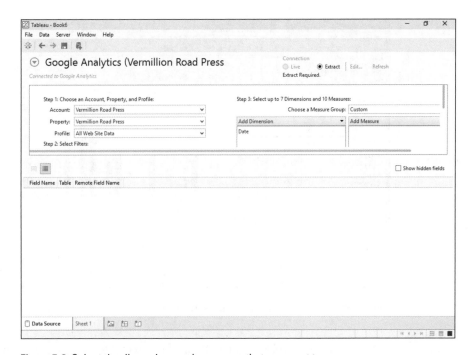

Figure 5-6: Select the dimensions and measures that you want to use.

After you've established the data connection, you can explore your data in Tableau Desktop. In most cases, functionality is the same regardless of data source.

Keeping Your Data Fresh

If your data analysis is based on an extract rather than a live connection, you may need to refresh the data to display current results. Otherwise, your analysis may quickly be out of date because an extract is a snapshot of the data as it was at the time of the extract rather than a continuously updating view of the data.

To refresh the extracted data, choose Data ➪ Refresh All Extracts from the main menu, as shown in Figure 5-7. This will refresh all the extracts for any data connections in your workbook. To refresh a single extract, click Data from the menu, choose the name of the data connection you want, then select Extract ➪ Refresh.

Figure 5-7: Refresh the extract to make sure that you're using up-to-date information.

You don't need to refresh the data in order to explore and analyze your data. Instead, do your design work first and then do the refresh just before you share your visualizations with other people.

6

Visualizing Data

In This Chapter

▶ Understanding Tableau's shelves and cards
▶ Hiding the data you don't need
▶ Working with filters
▶ Getting the visualization you want

*T*ableau is a master at enabling you to analyze and visualize your data. The desktop application makes it easy for you to connect with data sources and then use drag-and-drop techniques to produce quick views. But Tableau can do a whole lot more to help you create truly knockout visualizations when you take advantage of its shelves and cards, which are the subject of this chapter.

Using the Shelves and Cards

Tableau has several areas where you can drag and drop fields to create and enhance your visualizations. Figure 6-1 shows the Tableau Worksheet workspace with each of the shelves and cards empty and ready.

Don't get too hung up on whether a particular item is referred to as a shelf or a card. The objects in the workspace are called cards, which contain shelves that you can place fields on. For simplicity's sake, typically Tableau refers to the Columns and Rows shelves, Filter shelf, Pages shelf, and Marks card. The Marks card is unique and has one large shelf at the bottom that can hold many fields with different display options.

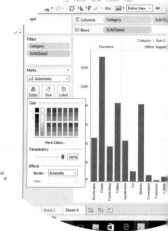

Because shelves and cards are key to creating effective Tableau visualizations, we cover each of them in detail in the following sections.

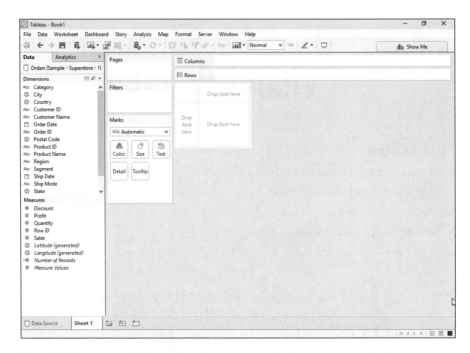

Figure 6-1: You use the shelves and cards to create and enhance your visualizations.

The Columns shelf

When you drag and drop something onto the Columns shelf, Tableau creates the columns of the chart. Exactly how the columns are created depends on whether you add a discrete dimension or a continuous measure to the shelf. As Figure 6-2 shows, adding a discrete dimension to the shelf — in this case, the State dimension — creates a header with labels for each of the members of that dimension.

Adding a discrete dimension to the view first will result in labels for the list of dimension members and automatically sets the mark type to text, as shown with "Abc".

Figure 6-3 demonstrates what happens when you add a measure to the shelf. In this case, adding the measure Sales creates a quantitative axis with a continuous range of values. The result is a bar showing the sum of sales along that axis.

By adding additional dimensions or measures to the shelves, you can add interesting elements to your view. For example, Figure 6-4 demonstrates what happens when you add multiple dimensions to the Columns shelf after placing a measure on Rows. In this case, Sub-Category was added after Category so Tableau created a new header with labels to display each sub-category within its associated category.

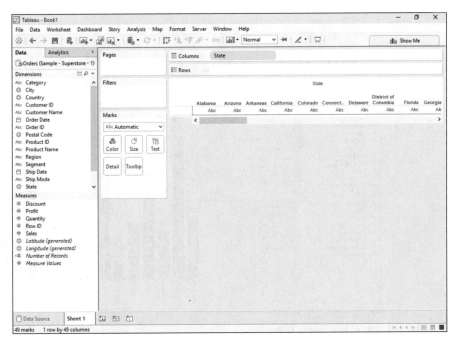

Figure 6-2: Adding a dimension creates labels based on the members of the dimension.

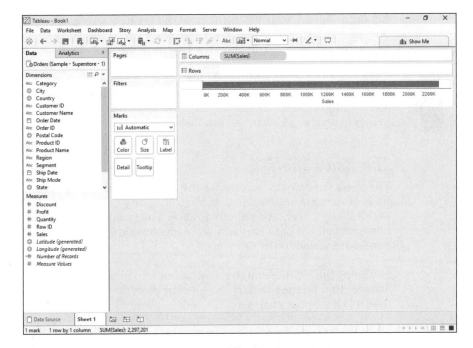

Figure 6-3: Adding a measure creates a numeric axis.

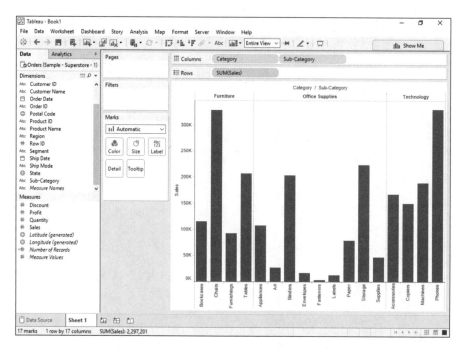

Figure 6-4: A second dimension adds a new header with labels.

Adding a second measure to columns will create a new axis next to the first one, each in its own row. As Figure 6-5 shows, Tableau adds a second axis below the original and displays the results as two separate bar charts.

If you want to add an additional measure to the same axis, you need to drop that measure onto the existing axis, rather than onto the shelf. For more on adding additional measures, see the "Using measure values and measure names in a view" sidebar, later in this chapter.

The Rows shelf

The Rows shelf works exactly like the Columns shelf except that the directions of the bars are swapped. In virtually every case, you'll actually use both of the shelves in creating a visualization. For example, Figure 6-6 shows a common vertical bar chart with a dimension added to the Columns shelf and a measure added to the Rows shelf.

Swapping the locations of the dimensions and measures (or clicking the Swap button on the toolbar) changes the direction of the bars, but otherwise doesn't affect your analysis.

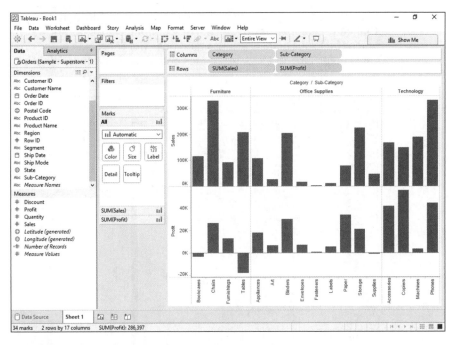

Figure 6-5: A second measure adds a second axis.

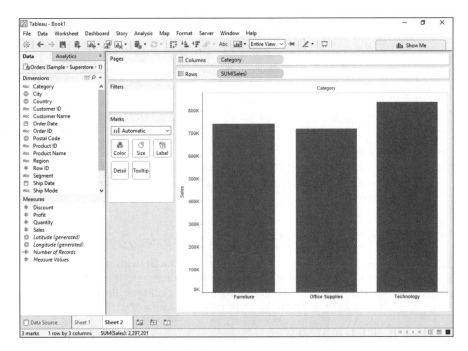

Figure 6-6: In most cases, you'll use both the Columns and Rows shelves.

Sometimes when you make certain changes in Tableau, it does something that can seem a bit mysterious. For example, Figure 6-7 shows what happens when the Profit measure is dragged onto the Sales axis in the chart. It substitutes fields named Measure Names and Measure Values. What's up with that?

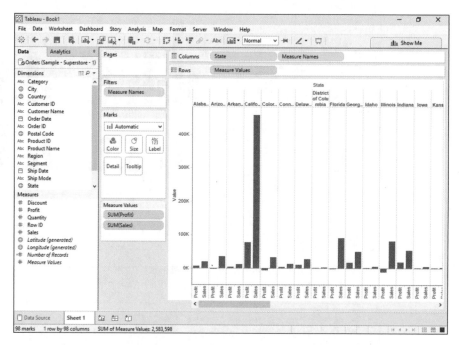

Figure 6-7: Tableau has its own generated fields that sometimes appear to help display multiple measures.

Measure Names and Measure Values fields are added to your visualization when you attempt to add more than one measure to the same axis. Sometimes you might do this on purpose, and sometimes you might do it quite by accident. For more on measure names and measure values, see the "Using measure values and measure names in a view" sidebar, later in this chapter.

Using a quick filter to exclude data

Often you may want to filter the data that's displayed in your view. Furthermore, you might want your audience to have the same option of filtering to what they would like to see. Quick filters offer the advantage of making it easy for you to change the view for yourself while also allowing you to provide a control for other users to select from.

Using measure values and measure names in a view

Measure values and measure names are Tableau-generated fields that serve as containers for more than one measure. When you create a Combined Axis view, these fields appear automatically, as does a Measure Values card that shows what fields are included.

Combined Axis charts have more than one measure on the same axis, which is useful for viewing multiple measures on the same scale. To give one example, you could drag your first measure to the Rows shelf, your second measure to the vertical axis, dropping it when you see the light green double-bar icon — then drag a dimension to the Columns shelf. If you were then to drag an additional instance of Measure Names from Columns to Color on the Marks card and edit the colors a bit, you'd end up with what you see below.

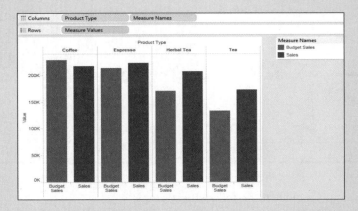

Another option when working with multiple measures in a view is to customize the Mark type for each measure. (You specify the Mark type used with the help of the Marks card, which splits into two sections to allow you to set Marks properties separately for each measure added to the view.) You could, for example, create a view with a line showing a target amount across several months, and a bar chart showing the actual attainment for those months, as shown in the figure below. These views with different mark types are known as *Combo* charts and allow you to easily compare two measures.

(continued)

(continued)

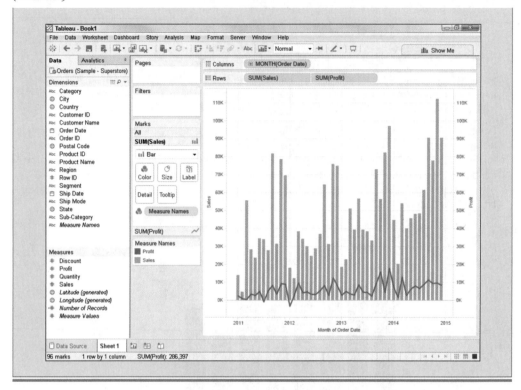

To apply a quick filter, follow these steps:

1. **Click the down arrow at the right side of the field on the shelf (or the Data pane) to display the field's pop-up menu, as shown in Figure 6-8.**

2. **Choose the Show Quick Filter option to display the quick filter.**

3. **In the pane that appears on the right side of the screen, deselect the check boxes for any data that you want to exclude from the visualization, as shown in Figure 6-9.**

When you add a worksheet to a dashboard, your quick filters will show up on that dashboard by default. That way, it's easy for people viewing the dashboard to filter the data themselves. In that case, you may find the long list of selections to be unsightly or that it takes up too much space. Change the display by clicking the drop-down arrow at the top of the Quick Filter pane and choosing something like Multiple Values (Dropdown).

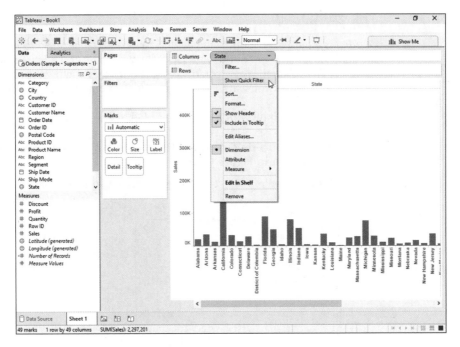

Figure 6-8: Display the menu for the field.

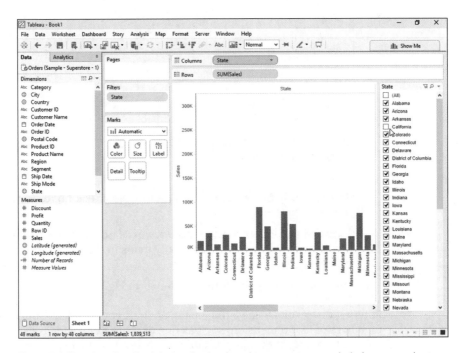

Figure 6-9: Deselect the check boxes for the data that you want to exclude from your chart.

The Filters shelf

Filtering is a method of controlling which rows of data are used to perform the analysis and appear in the view. An easy way to filter data in Tableau is by using the Filters shelf. When you drop fields onto this shelf, Tableau allows you to select the values you want to use from the data contained within that field.

To use the Filters shelf with a dimension, follow these steps:

1. **Drag and drop a field onto the Filters shelf to display the Filter dialog box, as shown in Figure 6-10.**

    In this case, we're using the Category dimension.

Figure 6-10: Use the Filter dialog box to choose the data that you want to use.

2. **On the dialog box's General tab, select the check boxes for the data you want to include.**

    Go ahead and select the Technology check box and leave the other check boxes deselected so that only items in the Technology category are included.

3. **Click OK to apply the filter, as shown in Figure 6-11.**

Filtering the results using a dimension enables you to select from distinct members of that dimension, such as one or more item categories. Filtering using a measure works just a bit differently because measures are typically numeric values.

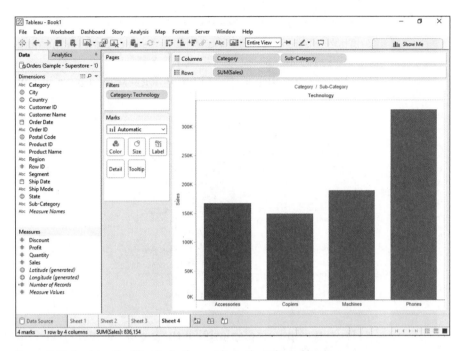

Figure 6-11: Applying the filter limits the results to the selected items.

To add a filter based on a measure, follow these steps:

1. **Drag a measure and drop it onto the Filters shelf to display the Filter Field dialog box, as shown in Figure 6-12.**

   In this case, use the Sales field.

Figure 6-12: Choose the type of operation for the filter.

2. **Select the type of operation you want to use from the list displayed.**

   Choose Sum to enable you to make a selection from the range of Sales values as aggregated by sum in the view.

3. **Click Next to display the Filter dialog box, as shown in Figure 6-13.**

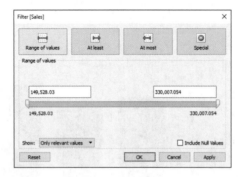

Figure 6-13: Choose the filter's conditions.

4. **From the options displayed at the top of the dialog box, select the type of filter you want.**

   In this case, choose the Range of Values option so that you'll have the greatest flexibility when you use the filter.

   Whatever option you choose, the dialog box refreshes to display controls specific to that option.

5. **If you want to specify the range of values now, use the sliders to set the range.**

   In this case, leave the sliders as is because you'll add a slider to the visualization as a quick filter.

6. **Click OK to apply the filter and return to the workspace.**

7. **Click the down arrow on the right side of the Sales field on the Filters shelf to display the menu shown in Figure 6-14.**

8. **Select Show Quick Filter to return to the workspace with the Sales Value slider added, as shown in Figure 6-15.**

9. **Drag the slider to control which sales appear in the visualization, as shown in Figure 6-16.**

As you drag the slider across the scale, Tableau updates the view so that only those values in the selected range are used. Because the filter is set to show a range of values, you can use both the upper and lower sliders to restrict the range.

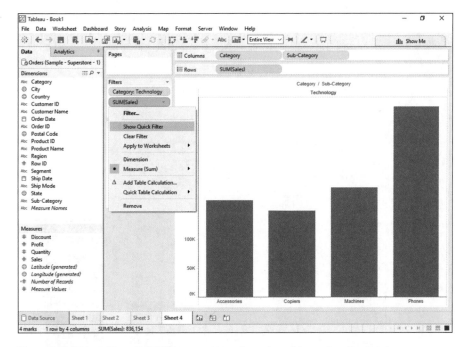

Figure 6-14: Select Show Quick Filter to add a sales value slider to the visualization.

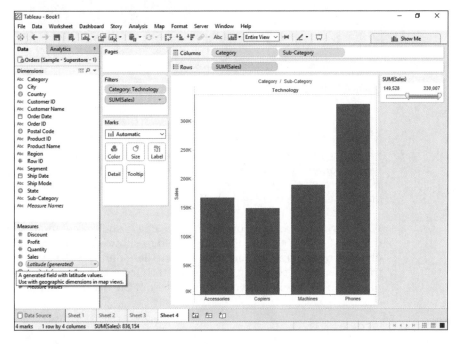

Figure 6-15: Use the slider to select which sales appear in the visualization.

TIP

The fields you add to the Filters shelf don't have to appear in the visualization. For example, using profit to filter the results of which sales are analyzed provides the option to only see profitable sales as opposed to the entire range of sales.

More options for filtering are covered in Chapter 14.

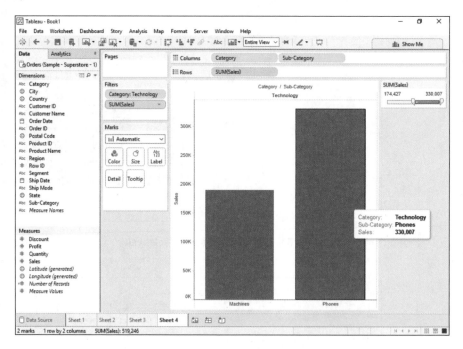

Figure 6-16: Drag the slider to control which values are used.

Pages shelf

Sometimes you may want to analyze your data based on the individual values contained within a field. This type of analysis can help you determine whether you're doing better over time. One handy way of doing this type of analysis is to use the Pages shelf.

While any field can be dropped into the Pages shelf, a common application (and best practice) is to add a Date field to show how your visualization changes over time. Drag and drop a Date field onto the Pages shelf in order to get the Page Control. In Figure 6-17, the Order Date dimension has been placed on the shelf, and you can select from the different years.

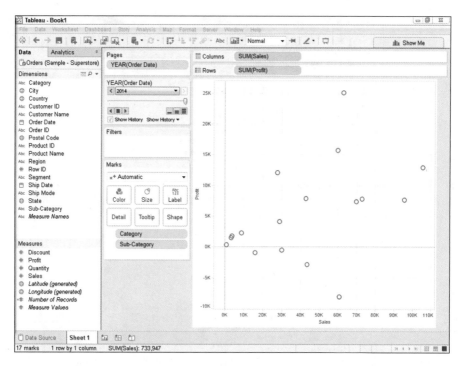

Figure 6-17: The Pages shelf enables you to flip through members of a field, changing and animating your analysis.

Hitting the Play button on the Current Page control animates the data by moving through field members. This shows you how your data is changing over time. To play the slideshow, use the playback controls that appear below the list box. Slideshows are probably more effective for fields that contain a large number of values, because Tableau only cycles through the values once (unless you choose Loop Playback from the drop-down menu) and doesn't automatically repeat when it reaches the end.

Another handy feature you can use is the Show History option for pages so that the view shows the values from previous pages in addition to the values for the current page. You can use the panel shown in Figure 6-18 to control how the history is displayed.

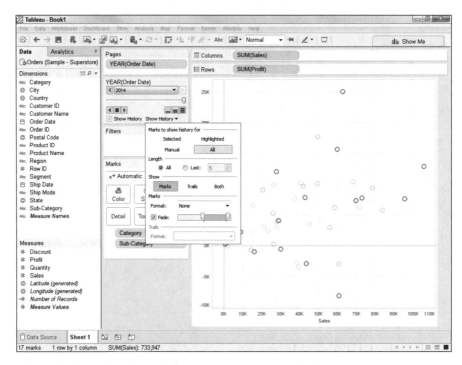

Figure 6-18: Enable the history display by clicking the Show History button.

You can choose the values you want to see (in this case, Order Date) using the drop-down list box, the arrows at the ends of the list box, or the slider below the list box in the Page control.

When the History display is enabled, Tableau displays the chart results from previous pages as faded marks. However, you can also add trails that are shown when selected, as shown in Figure 6-19. This enables you to compare the results across pages.

Marks card

The Marks card provides you with control over how the data is displayed in the view. The options on this card allow you to change the level of detail as well as the appearance of the marks without affecting the headers built by fields on Columns and Rows.

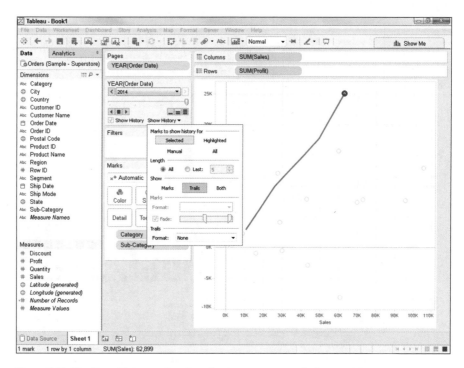

Figure 6-19: The Page history makes it easier to compare results from previous pages.

The Marks card drop-down menu is shown in Figure 6-20. You can select the type of mark that you want displayed by choosing one of the options from this list. In most cases, you will want to leave it set to Automatic and let Tableau decide on the best Mark Type for your visualization.

The Marks card is also where you can change the Mark properties with different options depending on your selected Mark type. The Color, Size, Detail, and Tooltip properties are always available; others that you might see are Shape, Angle, or Path. Clicking on a property will bring up options to customize the marks even further, as shown in Figure 6-21.

In many cases, more than one field can be used for a given encoding option — if you wanted both Sales and Profit as labels, for example. But if you want to add a second field to the Color control, you need to hold down Shift as you drag the field onto the control. The Size and Shape controls can only have one field added to them in a view.

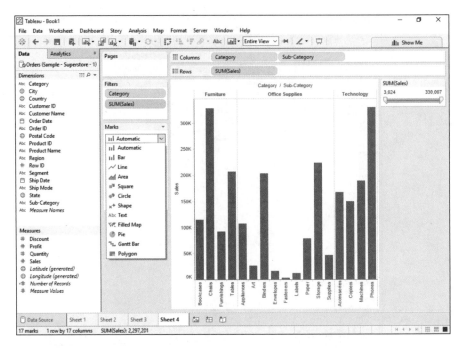

Figure 6-20: Use the list to choose the mark type.

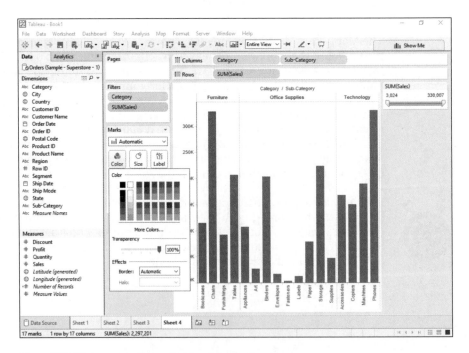

Figure 6-21: Click an encoding option to customize.

By default, Tableau displays a tooltip when you hover the mouse pointer over a data point in the view. This tooltip provides information about the data that's being displayed. You have the option of editing both the content and the appearance of the tooltips. To do so, click the Tooltip control to display the Edit Tooltip dialog box, as shown in Figure 6-22.

Figure 6-22: You can edit tooltips.

Modifying the View

After you've built your visualization, you may want to play around a bit more to modify the view so that it looks just right. A few small changes can help to make sure your visualizations are not only clear and easy to understand, but also visually stunning. Tableau provides options to format your view to better convey the information to your audience. We'll now look at several of these to get you started.

Fitting the space

One problem that you might encounter is that you have simply too much information to fit on the page. For example, if you want to show sales results by state, it's often difficult to show all 50 states on a single view. Several possible solutions might help:

✔ **Use a Fit option on the toolbar:** Use to determine the best fit for your dashboard. You'll find Fit options such as Fit Width, Fit Height, or Entire View in place of the default Normal.

✔ **Group to a higher level of detail:** Create a group of the low-ranking states to display their results in a single bar. (See the chapters in Part III for more information on grouping.)

✔ **Filter the results:** Add filters to reduce the amount of data that might not be necessary. By showing Quick filters you can also start with less and allow your user to choose more only if desired.

✔ **Use the Pages shelf:** You could page through single time periods by dropping a Date field to the Pages shelf.

✔ **Transpose:** It's often easier to read the axis labels when they're horizontal rather than vertical. In this case, you'd want to put the State field on the Rows shelf rather than the Columns shelf.

Adding annotations

You may also want to draw attention to a particular point, mark, or area in your view. One way to do this is to add an annotation to the view.

To add an annotation, follow these steps:

1. **Right-click the chart where you want to add the annotation.**

2. **Select Annotate from the menu that appears. (See Figure 6-23.)**

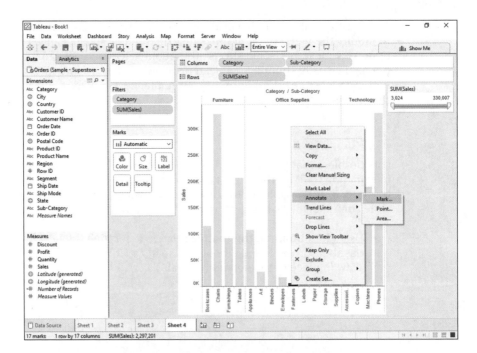

Figure 6-23: An annotation helps to bring attention to something important.

3. **Choose Mark, Point, or Area depending on whether you want to add the annotation to one of the marks, to a specific point, or to an area on the chart.**

   You need to click on a mark to add a Mark annotation, but the Point and Area annotations can be placed anywhere in the view.

4. **Create your annotation in the Edit Annotation dialog box, as shown in Figure 6-24.**

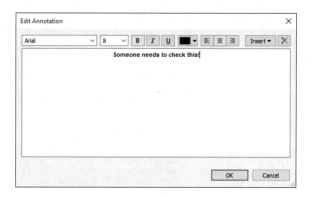

Figure 6-24: Create your annotation.

5. **Click OK to add the annotation to the chart.**

6. **If necessary, drag the annotation exactly where you'd like it to appear.**

The drag options are different for each annotation:

- ✔ **Mark annotations** have lines that always point to the mark; however, the text can move where you please within the view.

- ✔ **Point annotations** have lines and text that can move anywhere in the view as needed.

- ✔ **Area annotations** have a box that can be dragged around any section and is tied to the headers on the edges of the view.

Adding mark labels

Finally, you may want to display the actual values associated with the marks on the chart. (The default is not to show these values.) You can do so by clicking the Show Mark Labels button — the Abc button — on the toolbar, as shown in Figure 6-25. (Mark labels are simply labels that describe what the mark is showing.)

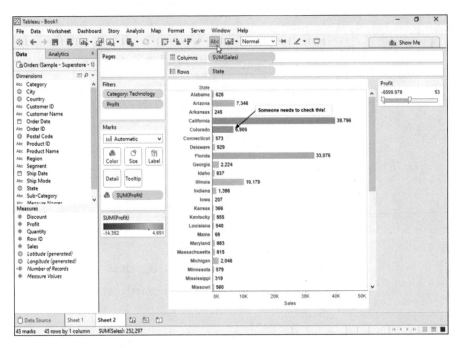

Figure 6-25: Mark labels make it easier to see the actual values.

Part III
Analyzing Data

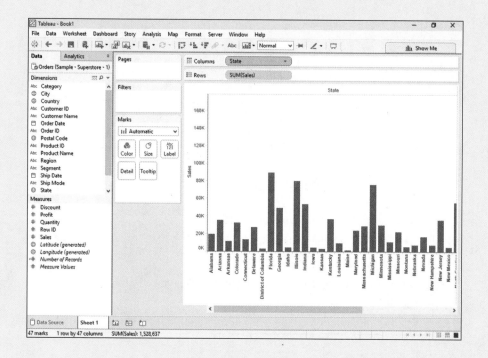

For more Tableau analysis tips and techniques, check out http://www.dummies.com/extras/tableau.

In this part . . .

- ✔ Master the Tableau Desktop environment.
- ✔ Look through the Tableau display options.
- ✔ Work with multiple worksheets.
- ✔ See how you can make dashboards work for you.
- ✔ Have your visualizations tell a story.

7

Understanding the Tableau Desktop Environment

In This Chapter

▶ Using the menus

▶ Getting to know the toolbar

▶ Organizing sheets

*W*ith any application, you may find it easy to simply use the basic features and not even think about how much more is out there. But in doing so, you shortchange yourself, so this chapter provides you with a deeper dive into some of the cool things you can do with Tableau.

With Tableau's highly visual environment, it's easy to create your data analyses and visualizations using drag-and-drop techniques. It's actually fun to see how much you can do just by clicking and dragging your mouse. But to take full advantage of Tableau, you'll want to also understand what you can do with the menus, the toolbar, and worksheet controls.

Looking at the Menus

If you've used a computer for any time at all, you've no doubt encountered menus. You know that you click the main categories such as File to display a drop-down list of commands that you can select. Tableau, of course, has a number of different menus that serve various purposes as you use the application. Many of the commands on these menus are quite familiar, but a number of commands will also be new to you. In the following sections, we take a look at Tableau's menus and highlight some of the commands you might find a bit unfamiliar.

File menu

Figure 7-1 shows the Tableau File menu that appears in the Worksheet workspace. (Note that the menu changes slightly between the Start page and Tableau workspace.)

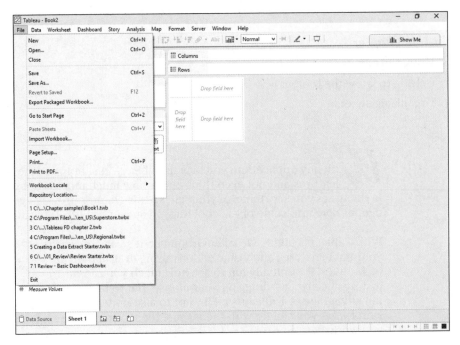

Figure 7-1: The File menu contains commands for interacting with files.

You no doubt already know what many of the commands on the File menu do. It's pretty obvious what things like New, Open, Close, Save, Save As, Page Setup, Print, Print to PDF, and Exit do, because these are commands that show up in tons of other applications. So we'll pass on those and take a look at some of the commands that are probably new to you:

✔ **Revert to Saved:** Sometimes it's inevitable that you need to undo a bunch of changes that you've made, especially if things didn't work out as you expected. You could use the Undo button to step back through the changes one by one, but using this command quickly brings you back to the last version of the workbook that you saved.

✔ **Export Packaged Workbook:** Using this command saves the workbook along with any local files that you've used as data sources in a single file. This command is especially handy when you want to share the workbook with other people who might not be able to access all those data sources from their computers. For example, you might need to share a Tableau workbook with someone who doesn't have access to your local network and file shares.

✔ **Go to Start Page:** You can use this command to return to the Tableau Start page, where you can open workbooks or connect to data sources.

✔ **Paste Sheets:** If you've put a lot of work into creating a Tableau worksheet, you can copy that worksheet from the workbook where you created it and then use this command to insert the sheet into your current workbook.

✔ **Import Workbook:** Rather than copying a single worksheet, you can use this command to bring everything from another Tableau workbook into your current workbook.

✔ **Workbook Locale:** If you work on an international team, you may have team members who create workbooks with different local settings such as currency or thousands separators. You can use this command to specify a specific locale for a workbook so that it will be compatible across the team.

✔ **Repository Location:** This command allows you to specify where various resources such as workbooks, data sources, styles, and so on are stored. If you are part of a team that collaborates using Tableau, you may want to have a shared repository on your network so that everyone can work with the same set of resources. But even if you work independently, it is good to know that this is where Tableau will default to opening and saving important files and settings.

Data menu

Figure 7-2 shows Tableau's Data menu as it appears in the Worksheet workspace.

Because you work with external data sources in Tableau, being able to define your connection to that data is vital to producing your analyses and visualizations. The commands you'll find on the Data menu include

✔ **New Data Source:** This command enables you to add an additional data source to your workbook.

✔ **Paste Data:** You can use this command to add data that you've copied from a source such as an Excel worksheet. You might find this handy if you only need part of the data in the worksheet or if you need to use data from another source that can produce comma- or tab-delimited data.

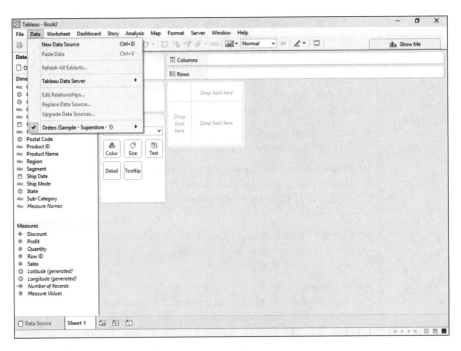

Figure 7-2: The Data menu enables you to work with data sources.

✔ **Refresh All Extracts:** If you have decided to create data extracts for multiple connections in your workbook, this option allows you to manually refresh multiple extracts at once. That way, you can make sure that you're using the latest data after you've finished setting up the view.

✔ **Tableau Data Server:** If you're connecting to a data source previously published to Tableau Server, you can refresh that data or append additional data from the server to your view.

✔ **Edit Relationships:** After creating multiple data connections, Tableau can relate them together by using common fields as links. This command enables you to create and modify relationships between data sources. The relationships become relevant when visualizing data from multiple sources in a single worksheet. (Tableau calls this *data blending*.)

✔ **Replace Data Source:** In some cases, you may have Tableau workbooks that you'd like to reuse with a different data source. This command provides a handy way for you to use a different data source without redoing the entire workbook.

✔ **Upgrade Data Sources:** If you've used Tableau for a while and have workbooks created in an earlier version, you can use this command to upgrade for better performance. (This option is specifically for Excel or text file data sources prior to Tableau Desktop version 8.2.)

Worksheet menu

The Worksheet menu, shown in Figure 7-3, enables you to do a number of useful tasks with Tableau worksheets.

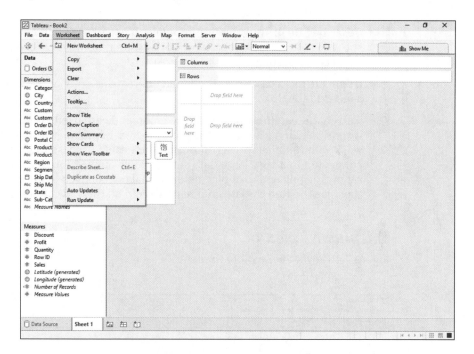

Figure 7-3: The Worksheet menu provides handy access to worksheet-related tasks.

Here's a quick look at the commands on the Worksheet menu:

- **New Worksheet:** This command simply duplicates the New Worksheet button and adds an additional worksheet to your Tableau workbook.

- **Copy, Export:** These commands enable you to copy an image, data, or cross tab to the Clipboard or to a file.

- **Clear:** You use this command to remove any changes you've made to various elements in the view. Although similar to the purpose of the Undo button, the Clear command doesn't require you to remove changes in the order they were applied.

- **Actions:** This command allows you to add customized interactivity to your worksheets. Options include highlighting and filtering dimension members in the view as well as providing hyperlinks that point to a web page or file location with the help of URL actions.

✔ **Tooltip:** You can use this command to modify the tooltips that appear when someone hovers the mouse pointer over the worksheet.

✔ **Show Title, Show Caption, Show Summary, Show Cards, Show View Toolbar:** These commands enable you to display or hide the various elements of the workspace.

✔ **Describe Sheet:** You'll find this command useful to document worksheets or to quickly understand worksheets that others share with you when collaborating.

✔ **Duplicate as Crosstab:** This command creates a copy of the worksheet as a text table.

✔ **Auto Updates, Run Update:** These commands are useful for controlling when Tableau performs updates of the data. Sometimes it's easier to work with updates turned off during the design process, such as when connected to a very large data set or a slow connection to the database. After dragging and dropping fields or making changes to filters, you can then use the Run Update command to refresh the view after you're done.

Dashboard menu

Figure 7-4 shows the Dashboard menu.

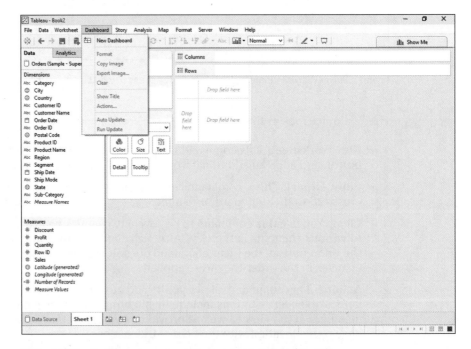

Figure 7-4: The Dashboard menu enables you to control dashboards.

As Figure 7-4 shows, the Dashboard menu is quite similar to the Worksheet menu, although without as many commands. The Dashboard commands only apply to Tableau dashboards, of course, but they function similarly to the same commands on the Worksheet menu.

Story menu

Figure 7-5 shows the Story menu.

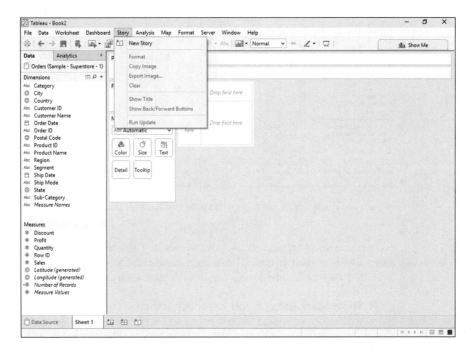

Figure 7-5: The Story menu enables you to control stories.

The Story menu is a virtual duplicate of the Dashboard menu with the exception of the Show Back/Forward Buttons command. As you can probably guess, this command enables you to show or hide the navigation buttons on a story page. The topic of creating stories is covered in Chapter 11.

Analysis menu

Figure 7-6 shows the Tableau Analysis menu.

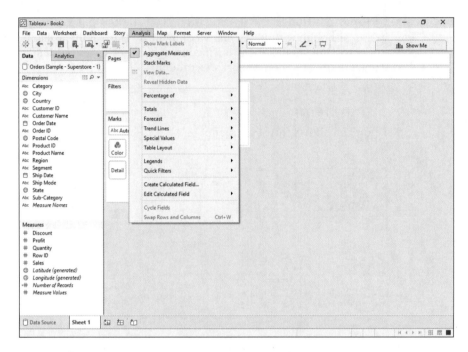

Figure 7-6: The Analysis menu provides powerful tools for data analysis.

When you want to customize your views in Tableau, the Analysis drop-down menu will be your friend. These commands enable you to take your worksheets to a whole new level of sophisticated analysis:

- ✔ **Show Mark Labels:** You use this command to show labels next to the marks on a chart. These labels can be the actual values associated with a measure, but you can show other types of labels, such as product names, too.

- ✔ **Aggregate Measures:** This command displays aggregate values such as the sum, the average, the median, and so on. (By default, Aggregate Measures is already turned on, so you would need to toggle it off if you wanted to disaggregate measures.) You can uncheck this option if you would like to show all the records rather than aggregates.

- ✔ **Stack Marks:** When you have bars or area charts with multiple dimensions, you'll notice the marks will stack on top of each other. This option allows you to have all the marks start from the same base line on your axis.

- ✔ **View Data:** Use this command to show the summary and underlying data in a given worksheet.

✔ **Reveal Hidden Data:** If you have hidden some of the data so that it doesn't appear on the chart, you can use this command to once again display that hidden data.

✔ **Percentage Of:** You can use this command to show the data as a percentage of the total data. You have several options to define which value you'd like to compare as the total.

✔ **Totals:** This command enables you to add subtotals and grand totals to the chart.

✔ **Forecast:** If you want to add a projection to your data over time, you can use this to create and customize forecasted values.

✔ **Trend Lines:** Trend lines are statistical models you can add to your view in order to quickly derive predictions, correlations, and other insights.

✔ **Special Values:** Some values such as nulls or unrecognized geographic values can't be plotted. You can use this command to choose whether Tableau indicates in the view that such values exist in the data.

✔ **Table Layout:** Use this command to control the display of empty rows and columns as well as field labels. You also have the option of selecting a few advanced options for the labels.

The #1 reason why people use the Table Layout menu is to get more than six dimensions as labels in the view without having them concatenate.

✔ **Legends:** Use this command to show or hide legends on your worksheet.

✔ **Quick Filters:** You can use this command to disable automatic updating when a Quick Filter is applied. You can also show/hide Quick Filters based off of active fields in the view.

✔ **Create Calculated Field:** Use this command to create a field whose value results from a calculation rather than from a field contained in the underlying data.

✔ **Edit Calculated Field:** When your data set contains calculated fields, you can use this command to easily locate and modify any calculations you have created.

✔ **Cycle Fields:** This option will swap the active fields to other locations in the workspace, which can be helpful if you want a quick way to reorganize your visualization to see what it looks like in a different configuration.

✔ **Swap Rows and Columns:** This button will simultaneously move fields found on Rows to Columns and vice versa.

Map menu

Figure 7-7 shows the Map menu.

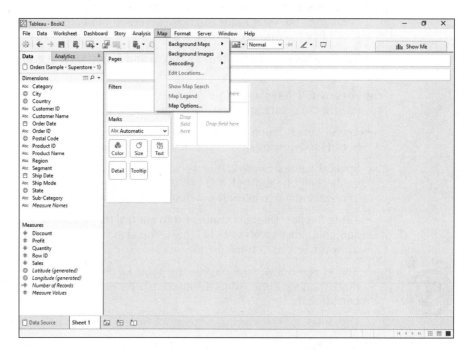

Figure 7-7: The Map menu enables you to control how Tableau displays geocoded data.

You can use the commands on the Map menu to change the maps, background images, and geocoding that Tableau uses to display geographical data. For example, if you have a custom map or want to base your geocoding on nonstandard political boundaries, you can use the commands on this menu to override the standard maps. (For more on your Map options, check out Chapter 8.)

Format menu

Figure 7-8 shows the Tableau Format menu.

Formatting is all about appearance as opposed to content, so changing the formatting options is a matter of personal preference. Nearly all selections will bring up the Format pane, which will cover the Data pane until you are done formatting and want to close it by clicking the "X" in the top corner.

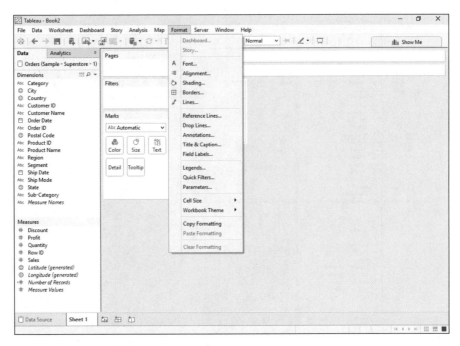

Figure 7-8: The Format menu enables you to control the appearance of your views.

If you'd like to have a consistent appearance throughout your workbooks, set the default formatting options before you begin building your views. You can change the formatting of pretty much any element of a view by right-clicking that element after you've created it, but any changes you make will only affect the selected element. By setting the defaults for fields at the start, every time you use that field throughout the workbook, it will have the same formatting (such as colors, sorts, dimension aliases, number format).

Server menu

Figure 7-9 shows the Server menu.

The Tableau Server menu provides access to options for sharing your Tableau workbooks. You can publish the workbook to Tableau Server and Tableau Online, or you can save to Tableau Public. Tableau Server is an on-premise application that you can install on a network server to share your data and visualizations. Tableau Online offers the same benefit but is hosted by Tableau Software and requires workbooks be connected to cloud-based datasources or that data be imported into Tableau Data Extracts. Tableau Public is a free product hosted by Tableau but is truly public in that any workbook can be searched for and explored by Tableau Public users.

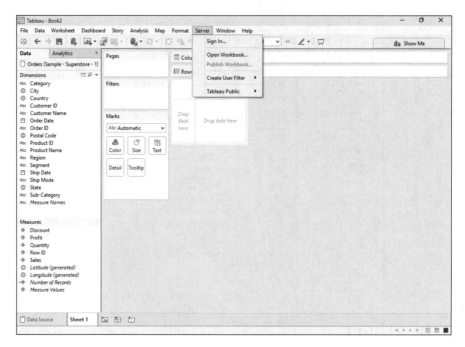

Figure 7-9: The Server menu provides access to Tableau Server options.

If you need to publish your Tableau workbooks to either Tableau Server or Tableau Online, you'll need to use the Professional Edition of Tableau Desktop, because the Personal Edition can only access Tableau Public.

The Server menu offers the following commands:

- ✔ **Sign In:** You'll need to sign in to authenticate your access to the server. Your system administrator provides the information you need to successfully sign in.

- ✔ **Open Workbook:** Use this command to access shared workbooks that are stored on the server.

- ✔ **Publish Workbook:** Use this command to publish a workbook to the server so that other users can share the workbook.

- ✔ **Create User Filter:** This command enables you to control which users can see which views — as well as which data within which view. For example, you might limit regional sales managers to viewing the results for their regions, thus preventing them from seeing the results from other regions.

- ✔ **Tableau Public:** This command enables you to open workbooks that are saved to Tableau Public, to save workbooks to Tableau Public, and to manage your Tableau Public profile.

Users can view the workbooks that you've saved to Tableau Public using a browser or Tableau Desktop Public Edition. This application allows users to create views, dashboards, and open downloaded workbooks; however, it cannot save any files locally as they all must be published to Tableau Public. (You can download the app for free from the Tableau Software website at www.tableau.com.)

Window menu

Figure 7-10 shows the Window menu.

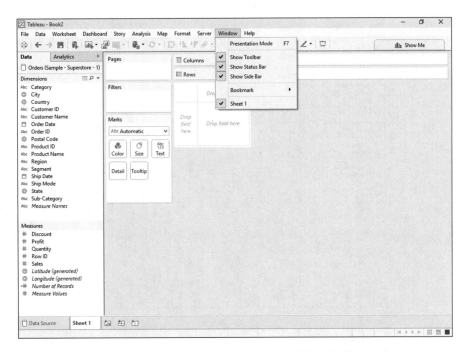

Figure 7-10: The Window menu enables you to control how Tableau is displayed.

You'll probably find the Presentation Mode command on the Window menu very useful if you need to do a live show featuring your Tableau workbook. This command displays the worksheets and dashboards in full-screen mode so that users won't see the various tools that normally appear in the work-space. Even without the shelves, cards, and panes, Presentation mode will still be responsive to user interactivity such as selections and highlighting.

The Bookmark command enables you to create a Tableau bookmark from a worksheet. Tableau bookmarks are worksheets that can be viewed in any Tableau workbook, so they're useful if you have worksheets that you need to reuse often in your visualizations.

Help menu

Figure 7-11 shows the Tableau Help menu.

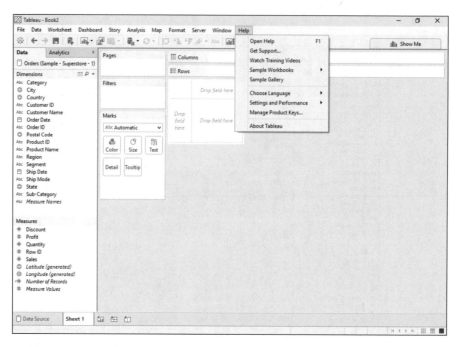

Figure 7-11: The Help menu provides access to help content and samples.

The Help menu is a pretty standard item for most applications, so it doesn't really need a lot of explanation. You may, however, want to check out the Settings and Performance menu to help test performance or manage integration with other tools. Also note that the About Tableau option will help you identify what version of the software you're on — handy if you ever need to file a support case or confirm the install of a new version.

TIP

If you've been using a trial version of Tableau, you can use the Manage Product Keys command to enter a product key when you license the application.

Making Use of the Toolbar

The Tableau toolbar provides quick access to a number of powerful tools that can make life a lot simpler with a single click. Figure 7-12 shows the buttons you'll find on the toolbar.

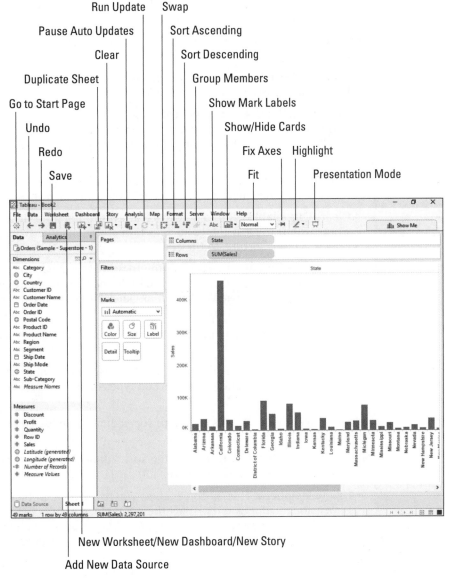

Figure 7-12: The toolbar has a bunch of handy tools.

The buttons include

- ✔ **Go to Start Page:** Returns you to the Tableau Start page, where you can connect to a data source or open a workbook.

- ✔ **Undo:** Each time you click this button, you move back one step through the history of the actions you've performed.

- ✔ **Redo:** If you go too far with the Undo Button, you can click this button to redo the step.

- ✔ **Save:** Click this button to save your workbook (make sure to do this often!).

- ✔ **Add New Data Source:** This button enables you to quickly add an additional data source to your workbook.

- ✔ **New Worksheet, New Dashboard, New Story:** This button enables you to quickly add a new worksheet, dashboard, or story to the workbook. You'll need to click the button's down arrow to add a dashboard or story.

- ✔ **Duplicate Sheet:** This creates an exact copy of the current worksheet that you can then modify as needed without starting from scratch.

- ✔ **Clear:** This enables you to quickly clear everything from the current worksheet or to clear things such as formatting, manual sizing, axis ranges, a filter, sorting, or the context.

- ✔ **Pause Auto Updates:** Use this button to prevent Tableau from updating information automatically as you build the view to improve performance. You can choose Worksheet or Quick Filter updates using the button's drop-down arrow.

- ✔ **Run Update:** Click this button to update the data when automatic updates are paused.

- ✔ **Swap:** This button transposes the fields between the columns and rows and changes the orientation of certain types of charts, such as bar charts.

- ✔ **Sort Ascending:** Use this button to sort a dimension list by ascending values of the associated measure.

- ✔ **Sort Descending:** Use this button to sort a dimension list by descending values of the associated measure.

- ✔ **Group Members:** This button enables you to create a group of selected Dimension members and display their combined results together. For example, if you have almost no sales in certain states, you might group them to show their combined sales as a single bar in a chart.

✔ **Show Mark Labels:** This button toggles the display of labels (typically representing values) associated with the marks on a chart.

✔ **Show/Hide Cards:** This button has a large drop-down list that enables you to display or hide the various elements of the view.

✔ **Fit:** This list box enables you to choose the zoom level for the current view so that you can control whether the entire view is visible in a single screen or whether you need to scroll to see everything.

✔ **Fix Axes:** This button locks the chart axes so that they cannot automatically grow or shrink.

✔ **Highlight:** You can use this button to add or remove highlighting from the chart.

✔ **Presentation Mode:** This button displays the view in full-screen mode without the Data pane, cards, and other elements of the workspace. It's very handy for giving live presentations — hence the name.

Organizing Sheets

Take some time to notice the three buttons that appear at the lower-right edge of the Tableau screen. These buttons can be pretty handy as you develop your Tableau workbook because they give you different ways to view and rearrange your worksheets.

Figure 7-13 shows a Tableau workbook in the default Show Tabs view. This view is very useful when you are creating your workbook.

Figure 7-14 shows the same workbook using the Show Sheet Sorter view. In this view, it's very easy to rearrange worksheets by dragging and dropping the thumbnails.

Figure 7-15 shows the Show Filmstrip view, which is essentially a hybrid of the other two views. You can also rearrange the workbook by dragging and dropping thumbnails in the filmstrip.

You can use Tableau's Presentation Mode command in either the Show Tabs or Filmstrip view.

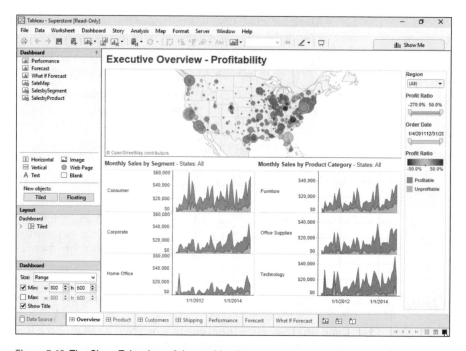

Figure 7-13: The Show Tabs view of the workbook.

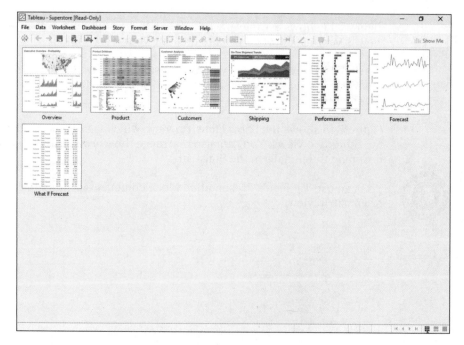

Figure 7-14: The Show Sheet Sorter view of the workbook.

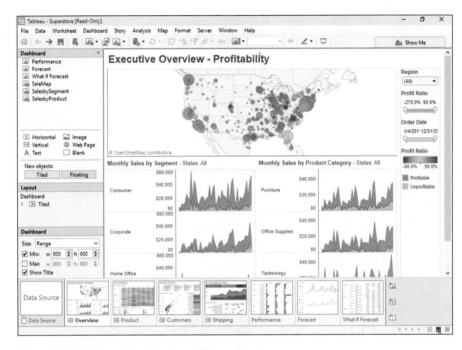

Figure 7-15: The Show Filmstrip view of the workbook.

Considering Data Display Options

In This Chapter
▶ Looking at the ways to display your data
▶ Double-checking your data
▶ Getting Show Me assistance

*W*hen you visualize data, it's important to use chart types that comple-
ment the data you are analyzing. Tableau offers a very broad range
of ways for you to visualize data, so you should be able to find the perfect
choice among the available offerings, or combine them to create something
new. This chapter shows you each of the chart options that you can choose
within the Show Me palette, and provides a deeper look at how Tableau's
Show Me tool can help make visualizing data easy.

Using Show Me

As you work on creating data analyses and visualizations in Tableau, you may want a little extra help in
deciding which chart types would be best for presenting that analysis. Tableau offers this extra help
through the Show Me tool shown in Figure 8-1.

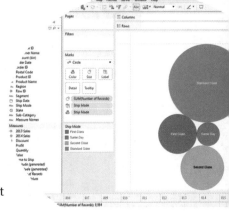

Show Me is a menu that sits at the right side of
the Tableau toolbar. You can display Show Me by
clicking the title bar. If you want, you can drag Show
Me to a different location on the Tableau screen and
close it any time by clicking the "X" in the upper-right
corner.

When Show Me is displayed, notice that some of the chart types are grayed
out, which means that those types are not recognized or recommended for
the dimensions and measures that you've selected. Even when a chart type is
grayed out, however, you can hover your mouse pointer over that type to see
the name of the chart type and the general requirements (which appear at
the bottom of the dialog box).

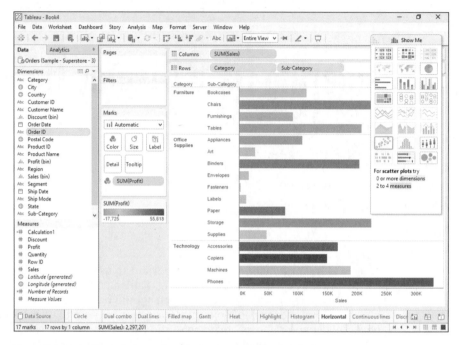

Figure 8-1: Show Me helps you choose chart types to fit your data.

If you choose one of the chart types and decide that you don't like it, click the Undo button and you'll quickly return to your previous chart type.

A really handy way to try out different chart types is to first click the Duplicate Sheet button on the toolbar so that you can experiment with a copy of your view rather than messing up a view that you've put a lot of work into.

Understanding the Chart Options in Show Me

Show Me will only suggest visualizations that work well with the fields you have selected. The following section discusses some of the charts that you can create with Show Me, and their relative strengths and weaknesses.

Area charts (continuous)

Area charts, such as the one shown in Figure 8-2, are commonly used to show values over a continuous time series. If you include more than one dimension in the chart, the values are stacked to indicate the totals, but sub-divided by color.

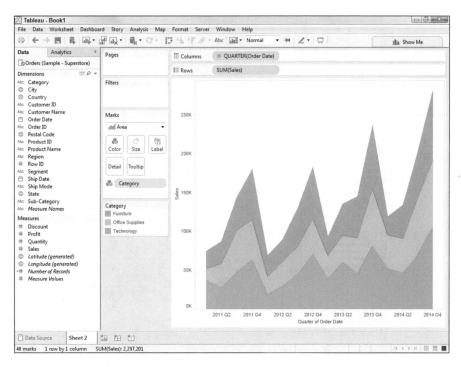

Figure 8-2: A typical continuous area chart.

Area charts (discrete)

Discrete area charts display the same information as continuous area charts, but break the data into a discrete time series, as shown in Figure 8-3. In this example, the time series is broken by years.

Box-and-whisker plot

Box-and-whisker plots show the distribution of values along an axis. The boxes show the middle 50 percent of the data, and the whiskers can be used to call out the full range of data or to identify outliers. Figure 8-4 shows a typical box-and-whisker plot.

Adding a second measure to a box-and-whisker plot you've set up using Show Me always creates a separate axis for the second measure.

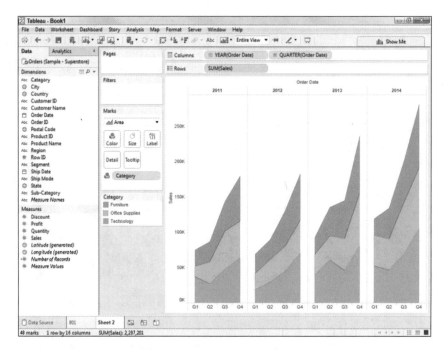

Figure 8-3: A discrete area chart uses separate axes.

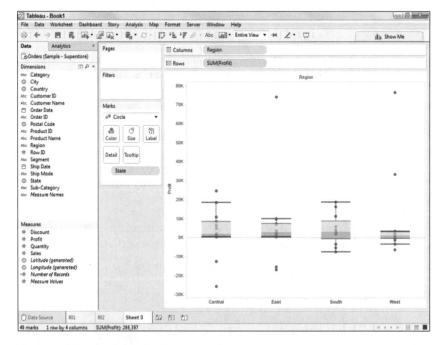

Figure 8-4: A box-and-whisker plot.

Bullet graphs

Bullet graphs are a variation of bar graphs that are typically used to compare the performance of a primary measure to one or more other measures. Figure 8-5 shows a bullet graph in which sales for the current year are compared to sales for the previous year across product categories and regions. Another common use case is to compare actual sales to target sales (or quota).

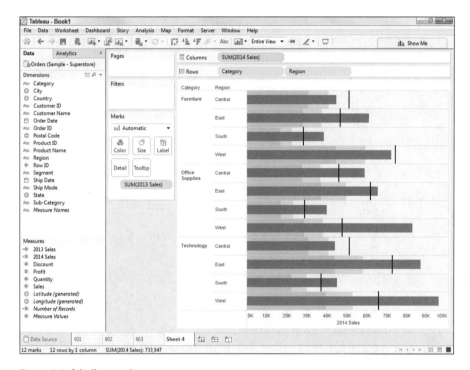

Figure 8-5: A bullet graph.

Circle views

Circle views show the value of measures using different symbols, as shown in Figure 8-6. With this type of view, you are generally looking at the distribution of data. In some cases, you may choose to add dimensions to your Marks card to show how you want to break up your values, or even choose to totally disaggregate your data by unchecking Aggregate Data under the Analysis menu.

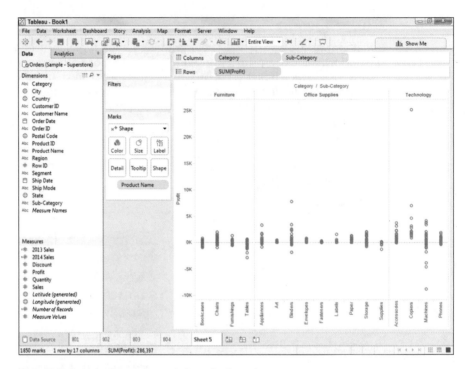

Figure 8-6: A circle view uses symbols to display values.

Dual combination

A dual combination chart uses multiple types of marks to display different information on the same sheet. Each measure can have its own axis and can be measured in totally different units (% to $), but the view still lets you see if the movement of the two measures seems to be related. For example, Figure 8-7 shows profits using bars measured by the left axis and discount as a line plotted against the right axis.

Dual lines

Dual lines charts display values as lines over time, as shown in Figure 8-8. Again, this chart allows you to have different axes with different scales and even different units of measure. After all, if your scale and units of measure are about the same, why not just have both measures share the same axis?

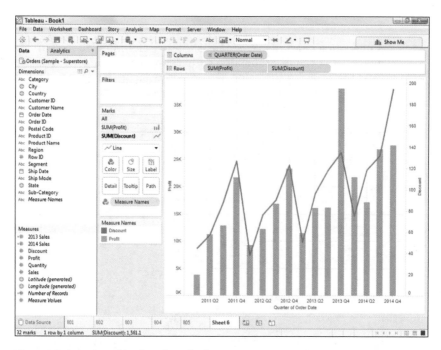

Figure 8-7: A dual combination chart displays measures using different types of marks.

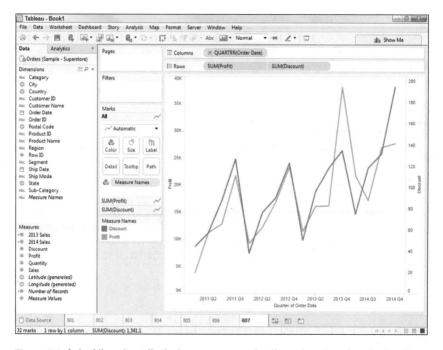

Figure 8-8: A dual line chart displaying measures using lines plotted against dual axes.

Filled maps

A filled map chart displays a map where different filled-in shapes are used to indicate the values associated with a geographic region. A color gradient is used to represent the value. For example, Figure 8-9 shows a filled map where the color of each state represents the sales for that state.

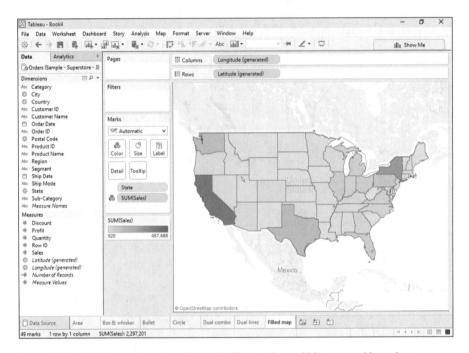

Figure 8-9: A filled map chart uses colors to indicate values within geographic regions.

If you need to use other maps, Tableau can connect to a Web Map Service (WMS) to use custom maps.

Gantt

Gantt charts help you visualize the stages of a project — for scheduling purposes, for example. The marks indicate the duration of the event. Figure 8-10 shows a Gantt chart that displays the length of time between when a customer placed an order and when that order was shipped.

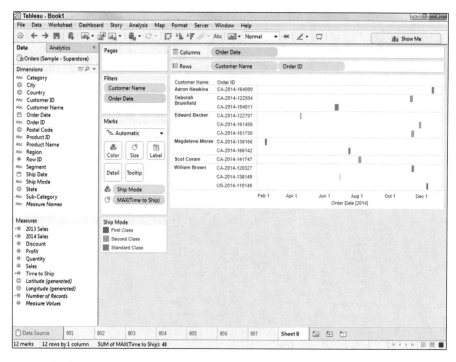

Figure 8-10: Gantt charts show the duration of events over time.

Heat maps

Heat maps enable you to compare data in various categories using different colors. For example, Figure 8-11 shows a heat map that displays both sales and profits broken down by customer segment, product category, and sales region. The heat map in this case uses different colors to indicate which areas of business are profitable and which are not, and then uses the size of the square to represent the amount sold. It is easy to spot where sales are high (a large square) and where we are losing money (an orange square).

Highlight tables

Highlight tables are similar to heat maps in that they display data in various categories using different colors, but highlight tables also include the actual data values in the chart. For example, Figure 8-12 shows a highlight table that displays a table providing profit information broken down by the same dimensions as the heat map in Figure 8-11, except the numbers are high-lighted by the profit values to draw extreme values to your attention.

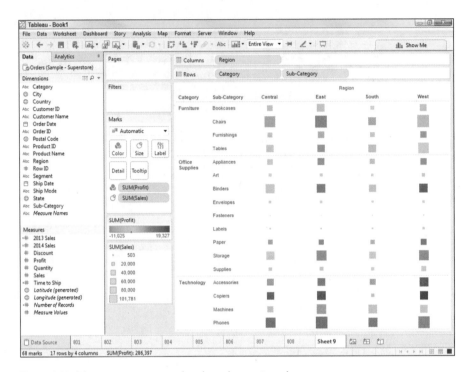

Figure 8-11: A heat map compares data in various categories.

Histogram

Histograms (also known as *frequency tables*) show the distribution of values as they fall into various intervals (or bins). Figure 8-13 is a histogram showing the distribution of scores on an exam.

Horizontal bars

Horizontal bar charts display values using the length of the bars. Figure 8-14 shows a horizontal bar chart with sales broken down by category and sub-category.

We could have added the Profit measure to Color on the Marks card so that the colors of the bars indicate how profitable the sales in each sub-category were.

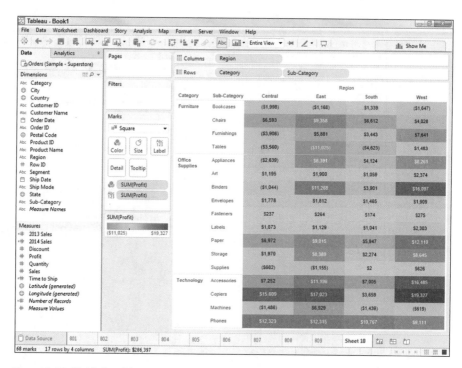

Figure 8-12: Highlight tables compare data in various categories using colors and also by displaying the actual data values.

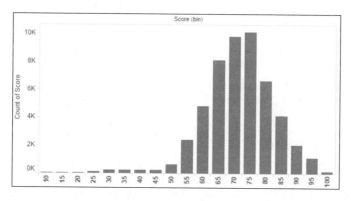

Figure 8-13: A histogram displaying the distribution of scores on an exam.

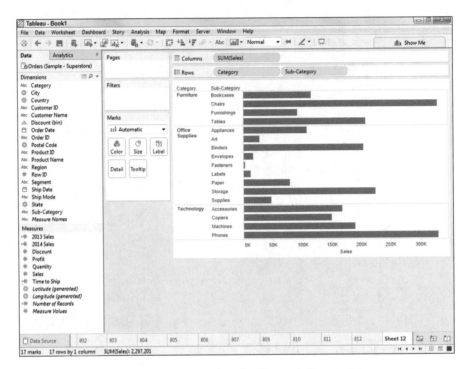

Figure 8-14: A horizontal bar chart uses the length of bars to indicate values.

TIP

You can click on the Swap button on your toolbar. And now you have a Vertical bar chart!

Lines (continuous)

Continuous line charts connect the data points using lines that make it easier to see trends over time. Figure 8-15 shows sales by week over several years.

Lines (discrete)

Discrete line charts also connect the data points using lines, but as Figure 8-16 shows, the lines don't have to connect across the entire chart. In this case, sales can be compared within a date hierarchy, breaking the lines at each next date part. Sometimes the use of discrete time series can help us see seasonality more easily. For example, in Figure 8-16, it is easier to see how sales tend to change by quarters within years than it is in Figure 8-15.

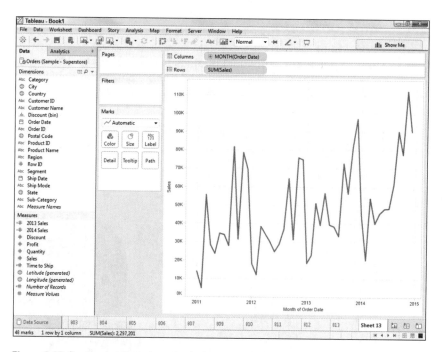

Figure 8-15: Continuous line charts make it easy to see time trends in the data.

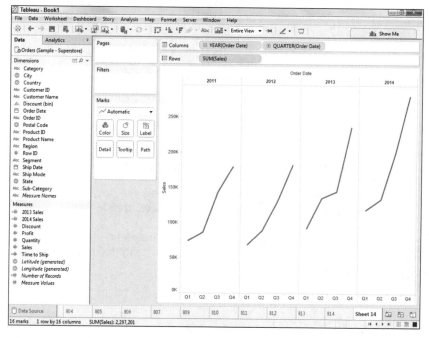

Figure 8-16: Discrete line charts make it easy to see trends and breaks in the data.

Packed bubbles

Packed bubble charts display data as a cluster of circles. You use dimensions to define the individual bubbles and measures to define the size of the bubbles. Figure 8-17 shows a packed bubble chart that depicts the number of items shipped (the size of the circles) broken down by ship mode.

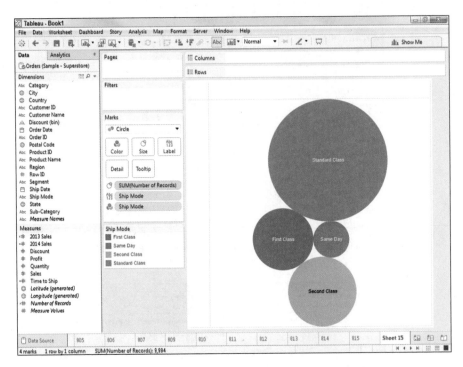

Figure 8-17: Packed bubble charts use circles of different sizes and colors to display data.

Pie charts

Pie charts show values as a percentage of the total. For example, Figure 8-18 shows the sales in each region (shown as a color) as a percentage of the total sales. In this case, both Region and Sales were dropped onto Label on the Marks card so that the individual pie slices are identified.

As shown in Figure 8-18, it's sometimes helpful to change the label format on numeric values (such as sales as currency) to make those values easier to understand.

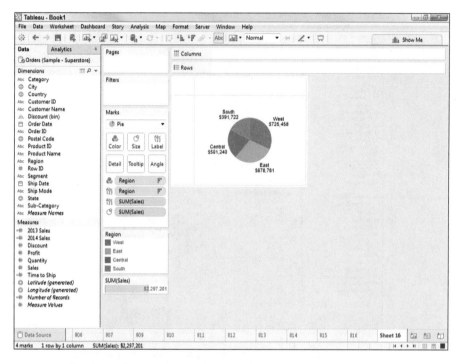

Figure 8-18: Pie charts display a visual representation of percentage.

Scatter plots

Scatter plots enable you to visualize relationships between numeric variables. To create a scatter plot, you need to place at least one measure on each of the Columns and Rows shelves. Then you can add one or more dimensions to the Marks card to tell Tableau how to sub-divide the data. Alternatively, you can choose to disaggregate all of your data. The purpose of a scatter plot is to visually determine whether there is a relationship between your measures. In the sample scatter plot shown in Figure 8-19, we are attempting to see whether profit tends to increase as the size of a sale increases.

Side-by-side bars

Side-by-side bar charts display related data as individual bars, as shown in Figure 8-20. In this case, the bars are color-coded to indicate which measure they represent.

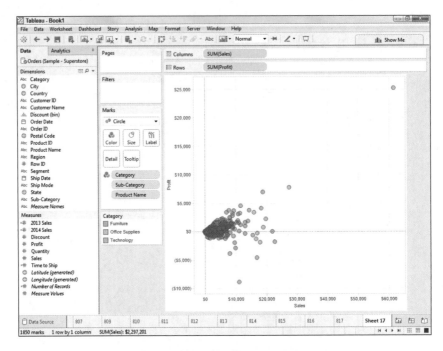

Figure 8-19: Scatter plots display relationships between measures.

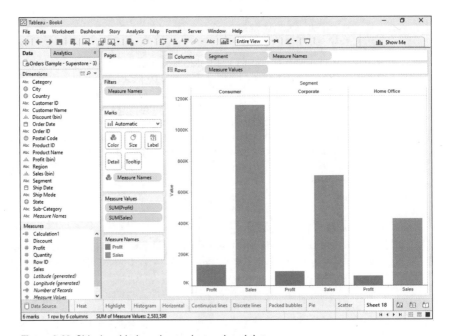

Figure 8-20: Side-by-side bar charts show related data.

Side-by-side circles

Side-by-side circles charts display related data as color-coded circles, as shown in Figure 8-21. This particular visualization is showing the distribution of a measure across one or more dimensions. In this case, we can see how the Total Sales measure is distributed by Product Category over the past several years. By placing Category on the Color shelf, we are color-coding to make the visualization easier to interpret. By placing State on the Marks card, it implies we will see one mark for each state in each Category and Year pairing.

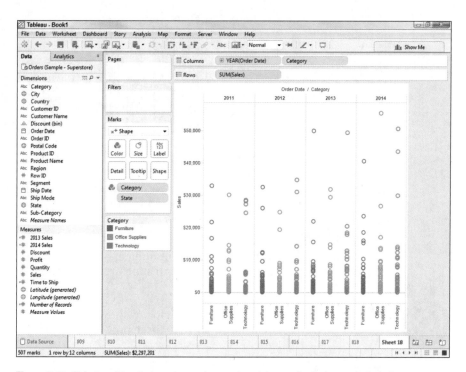

Figure 8-21: Side-by-side circles charts show related data using color-coded circles.

Stacked bars

Stacked bar charts show how individual elements contribute to a total. Figure 8-22 shows a stacked bar chart that breaks down sales by category and segment, with sales for each region shown as a different color.

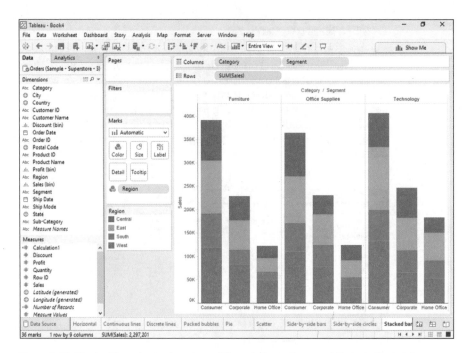

Figure 8-22: Stacked bar charts show how different dimensions contribute to the total.

Symbol maps

Symbol maps show values using a geographical map, as shown in Figure 8-23. In this case, the sales in each state are indicated by the size of the circle.

You can even use pie charts as your shape to show, for example, how the sales in each state break down into the three product categories.

Text tables

Text tables display values as numbers in a table, as shown in Figure 8-24. In this case, the view shows profit, sales, and discount broken down by region and category.

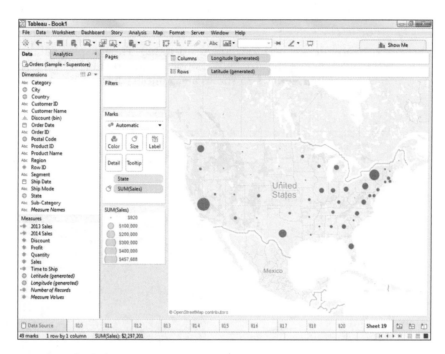

Figure 8-23: Symbol maps show results plotted on a map.

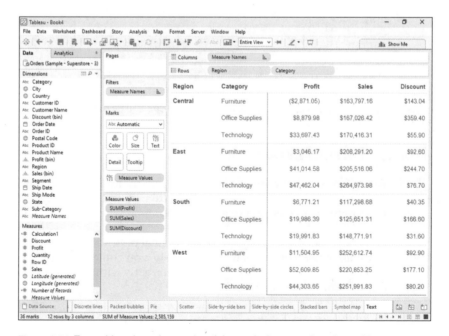

Figure 8-24: Text tables show the results of the analysis as numbers in a table.

Treemaps

Treemaps show a part-to-whole relationship. They display data in nested rectangles, where the size and position of each rectangle is determined by a measure value. Figure 8-25 shows an example where sales are broken down by region, state, and city.

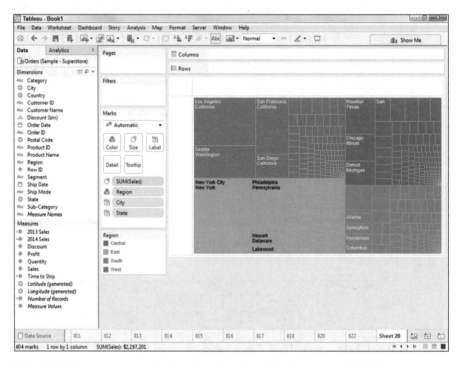

Figure 8-25: Treemaps use rectangles of varying size and color to represent values.

Viewing Your Data

Tableau turns your data into a visual representation, but sometimes, you need to view the actual raw data. Perhaps a result in the analysis just doesn't seem right, or maybe you're just curious about what's going on underneath.

You could, of course, go back to the original data source to have a look at the raw data outside of Tableau. Alternatively, you could click the Data Source tab and view the records you are using directly within Tableau, as shown in Figure 8-26.

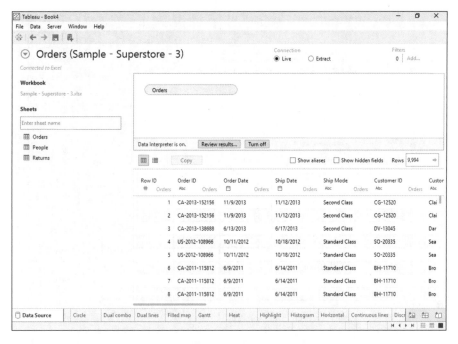

Figure 8-26: You can view the underlying data source within Tableau.

Although you can view the entire underlying data source, as shown in Figure 8-25, doing so is a rather cumbersome way of looking at the data. A typical database table likely contains a number of fields as well as a bunch of records that you're probably not using in a typical analysis and visualization. Fortunately, Tableau makes it easy for you to focus on just the data that you're actually using in a view. The next section shows you how.

Examining the data used in a view

To view just the data that's actually being used in an analysis you've created in Tableau, follow these steps:

1. **Open the worksheet whose data you want to view by clicking its tab along the bottom of the Worksheet tabs.**

2. **From the main menu, choose Analysis ⇨ View Data to display the Summary tab of the View Data dialog box, as shown in Figure 8-27.**

3. **Click the Underlying tab in the box's lower-left corner to display the raw data that's used to produce the view, as shown in Figure 8-28.**

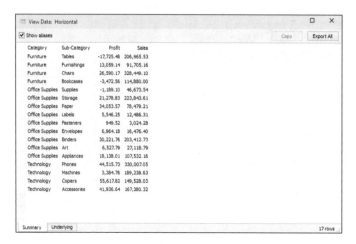

Figure 8-27: The Summary tab displays the summarized data shown in the view.

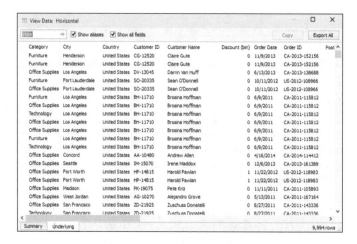

Figure 8-28: The Underlying tab displays the raw data shown in the view.

4. **For a less confusing view that only displays the actual fields that are being used in your analysis, deselect the Show All Fields check box in the toolbar at the top, as shown in Figure 8-29.**

5. **Click the Close button in the upper-right corner of the dialog box to return to the worksheet.**

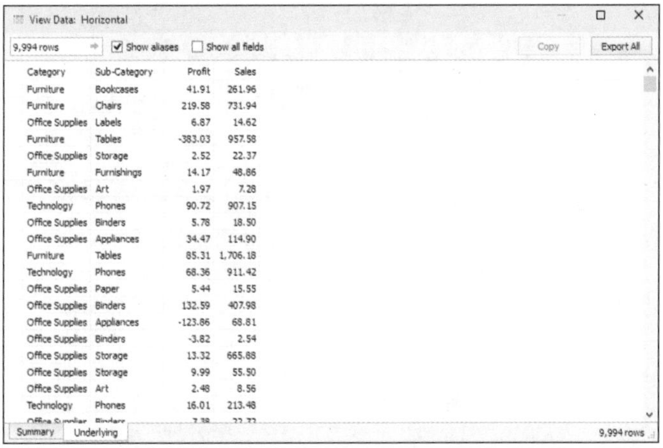

Figure 8-29: Deselect the Show All Fields check box to limit the data to what's actually being used.

Examining a subset of the data

You can also focus on a subset of the data that's associated with one or more of the marks in a view. You may find this useful if a particular result appears to be questionable. For example, a particular bar may be longer than you expect it to be and you want to see what individual values make up that bar.

To view a subset of the data, follow these steps:

1. **Open the worksheet whose data you want to view by clicking its tab.**

2. **Right-click the mark that you want to examine.**

   You can also do this from the tooltip command buttons that show up when you normally click on a mark.

3. **From the contextual menu that appears, choose the View Data command, as shown in Figure 8-30.**

4. **In the View Data dialog box that appears (see Figure 8-31), click the Underlying tab.**

5. **Scroll through the subset of records that are displayed, as shown in Figure 8-32, to verify that the data appears to be correct.**

6. **Click the Close button in the upper-right corner of the dialog box to return to the worksheet.**

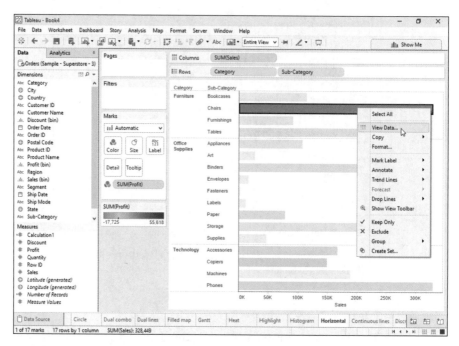

Figure 8-30: Choose the View Data command.

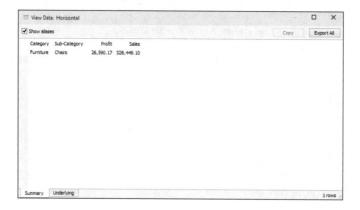

Figure 8-31: The dialog box now shows only the selected data.

Category	Sub-Category	Profit	Sales
Furniture	Chairs	219.58	731.94
Furniture	Chairs	-1.02	71.37
Furniture	Chairs	-15.15	212.06
Furniture	Chairs	17.10	89.99
Furniture	Chairs	7.10	319.41
Furniture	Chairs	-15.22	213.12
Furniture	Chairs	-114.39	831.94
Furniture	Chairs	33.22	301.96
Furniture	Chairs	-8.58	600.56
Furniture	Chairs	-9.16	81.42
Furniture	Chairs	585.55	1,951.84
Furniture	Chairs	51.48	457.57
Furniture	Chairs	-24.86	1,740.06
Furniture	Chairs	21.26	340.14
Furniture	Chairs	-11.34	396.80
Furniture	Chairs	-28.27	161.57
Furniture	Chairs	43.84	389.70

Figure 8-32: You can scroll through the selected data to verify it.

You can select more than one mark whose data you want to view by holding down the Control key while making your selection. You can also select subsets of data that you want to view by selecting the items on the chart axes. For example, to view all the items in the Office Supplies category, right-click Office Supplies on the chart axes and then choose the View Data command.

Category	Category	Category	Category
■ Furniture	■ Furniture	■ Furniture	■ Furnitu
■ Office Supplies	■ Office Supplies	■ Office Supplies	■ Office
■ Technology	■ Technology	■ Technology	■ Techno

Category	Category	Category	Category
■ Furniture	■ Furniture	■ Furniture	■ Furniture
■ Office Supplies	■ Office Supplies	■ Office Supplies	■ Office Suppl
■ Technology	■ Technology	■ Technology	■ Technology

9

Adding Worksheets

. . . .

In This Chapter

▶ Understanding the value of worksheets

▶ Getting some worksheet organization

. . . .

*W*orksheets are a key element in Tableau. While every analysis you create is based on the data you've connected to, you will visualize that data within the worksheet. This chapter takes a closer look at worksheets and provides some helpful information to enable you to make the most of them.

Seeing Why Multiple Worksheets Are Useful

Every new Tableau workbook begins with a blank worksheet named Sheet 1. After you've connected to a data source, that worksheet is ready for you to begin creating a view of your data, as shown in Figure 9-1.

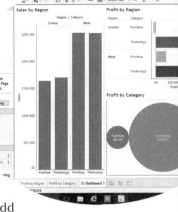

A blank worksheet is like a fresh canvas for an artist — it's ready to hold your next masterpiece. You can build anything from a simple bar chart to a scatter plot complete with trend lines and confidence bands.

As flexible as Tableau worksheets are, each one can only show one view of a subject at a time. You can't, for example, show a stacked bar chart and a symbol map on a single worksheet at the same time. If you want to see both on the same page, you need to create a dashboard and add the visualizations from your worksheets to the dashboard.

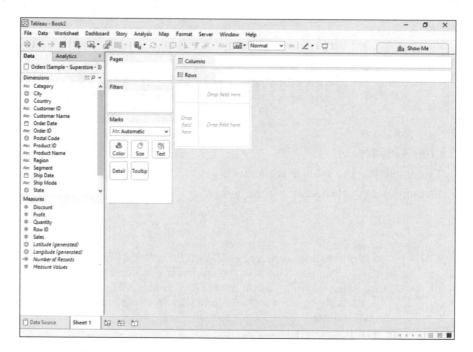

Figure 9-1: Tableau always creates a blank worksheet when you open a new workbook.

You can only create visualizations on worksheets, not on dashboard or story pages. You can use — but not create — those visualizations on dashboards and stories.

To get a better feel for how you can put multiple worksheets to use, let's take a look at a quick example. Figure 9-2 shows sales by state plotted on a geographic map.

Next, we've created another worksheet (see Figure 9-3) that shows total sales for each year.

Finally, Figure 9-4 depicts a horizontal bar chart with sales sub-divided by product category and sub-category.

Now that these three visualizations exist, we'll add them to a Tableau dashboard so that it's easier to share a more complete picture of sales with other people. Figure 9-5 shows the completed dashboard, which clearly shows the value of having multiple related worksheets in the same dashboard.

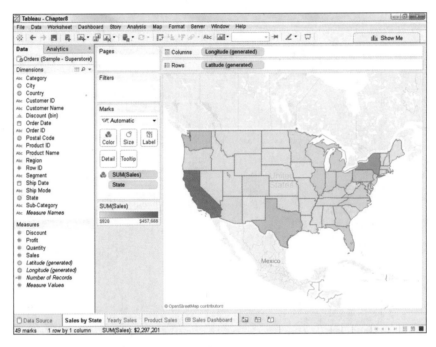

Figure 9-2: This worksheet shows sales by state.

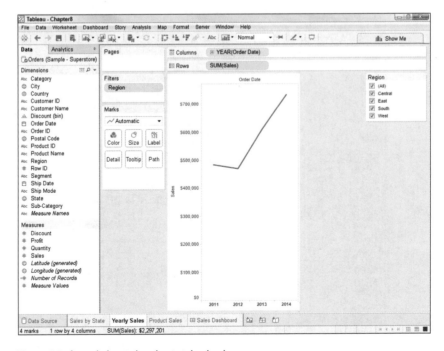

Figure 9-3: A worksheet showing total sales by year.

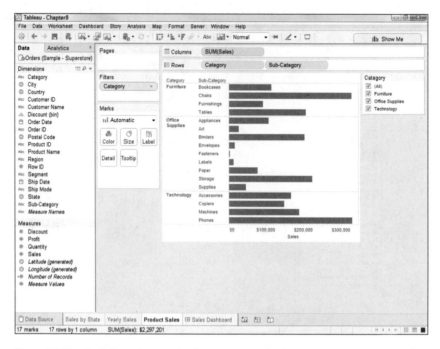

Figure 9-4: The final chart shows sales by category and sub-category.

Figure 9-5: The dashboard uses all three visualizations to tell the story of sales.

In this example, the dashboard also includes quick filters (covered in Chapter 6) for region and category as well as legends to explain the content by specifying the meaning assigned to the colors. Figure 9-6 shows what happens when both the Region and Category filters are selectively applied. Now, only the results that match the filter criteria are displayed.

Figure 9-6: The results are now filtered.

Although you could keep each view on its own worksheet and click between them, this example provides a clear picture about the usefulness of having all three visualizations available at the same time. Not only are you able to tell a more complete story, but the interactivity allows viewers to explore the data for themselves.

It is important to account for the "scope" of your quick filters. Which sheets do you want the filter to affect? See Chapter 6 for more information about the scope of filters.

Any quick filters that you create and apply work in both directions between worksheets and dashboards. That is, if you select a specific region or category on the quick filter shown on a dashboard, it also applies to any worksheets that have the same filter. Likewise, if you select a specific region on the quick filter on a worksheet, the dashboard will also display the same selection. (See Chapter 6 for more on using filters.)

Naming and Organizing Worksheets

As you use Tableau, you'll almost certainly be creating a number of worksheets. To make your life a little bit easier, you'll want to name and organize those worksheets.

Naming worksheets

Tableau's default naming method for new worksheets you create is to call them Sheet 1, Sheet 2, Sheet 3, and so on. Although this is a logical way for Tableau to name the sheets, it probably won't be very helpful when you want to add those visualizations contained on the worksheets to a dashboard or story. You'll find it a lot more useful if you give each worksheet a descriptive name.

To name your worksheets, follow these steps:

1. **Right-click the worksheet tab in the lower portion of the screen to display the tab's pop-up contextual menu.**

2. **Select Rename Sheet from the menu, as shown in Figure 9-7.**

3. **Enter the name that you want to use for the worksheet into its (now editable) tab, as shown in Figure 9-8.**

4. **Press Enter to apply the name.**

You can use any name you like for your worksheets, but you'll find it most useful if you give them descriptive names relating to the content that's included on the worksheet. Doing so will make it much easier for you when you want to add those visualizations to a dashboard or to a story.

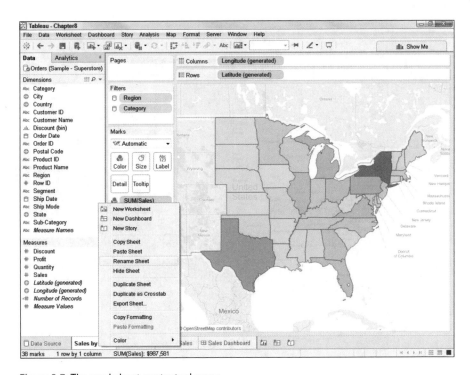

Figure 9-7: The worksheet contextual menu.

Organizing worksheets

As you build larger Tableau workbooks that contain many worksheets (and possibly dashboards and stories), you may discover that keeping track of all the worksheets gets to be a little confusing. Fortunately, Tableau gives you a couple of tools to help you stay organized.

Figure 9-9 shows Tableau's Sheet Sorter view, which you can access by clicking the Sheet Sorter button near the lower-right corner of the window. In this view, you can reorder worksheets by dragging and dropping.

You can also use Tableau's Filmstrip view, which displays the worksheets and dashboards as thumbnails at the bottom of the workspace, to reorganize your content using drag-and-drop techniques. In most cases, though, it's easier to use Sheet Sorter view when you want to reorganize things.

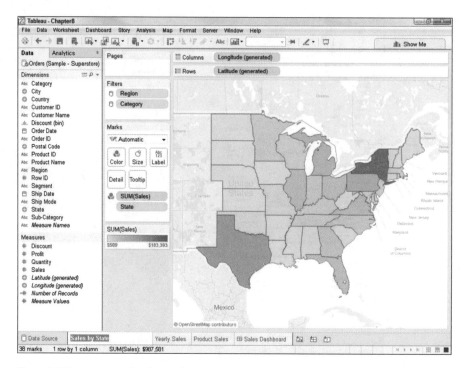

Figure 9-8: Enter a name for the worksheet.

If you don't want viewers to see the individual worksheets, you can also hide them by right-clicking the worksheet tab and selecting Hide Sheet from the contextual menu that appears. If you want to hide all the worksheets and only leave dashboards and stories visible, right-click a dashboard tab and choose Hide All Sheets from the pop-up menu.

After you've hidden Tableau worksheets, it can be a little confusing figuring out how to get them back. To unhide all the hidden worksheets, right-click a dashboard tab and choose Unhide All Sheets from the pop-up menu. Worksheets that you unhide will appear as tabs following the Dashboard tab regardless of where they were before they were hidden.

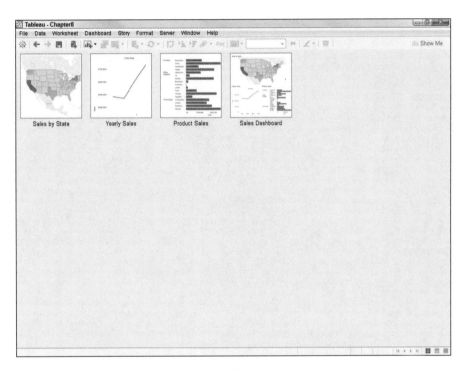

Figure 9-9: Use the Slide Sorter view to reorganize your worksheets.

10

Creating Dashboards

● ●

In This Chapter

▶ Seeing the value in dashboards

▶ Creating dashboards

▶ Keeping tabs on the dashboards you create

▶ Making sure that your dashboards are easy to use

▶ Adding actions

● ●

*T*ableau is a great tool for analyzing data and creating visualizations, but it's also helpful when you want to share those analyses with other people. Dashboards make it possible for you to bring together several views and let your audience interact with a "big picture" view of the results. This chapter takes a deeper look at both how and why you'll find dashboards so useful in Tableau.

Understanding the Purpose of Dashboards

It's pretty rare that a single picture can tell an entire story. A single Tableau worksheet generally can't give a completely comprehensive analysis to answer a question you are asking of your data, because a single view simply has to leave too much out.

Tableau dashboards make it easy to combine several worksheets together and gain a more comprehensive view of your data. For example, Figure 10-1 shows a sample dashboard that enables a viewer to examine sales and profits according to geographical regions while selecting either all categories of products or individual categories. The separate views contained in the dashboard make it much easier to understand where the company can improve.

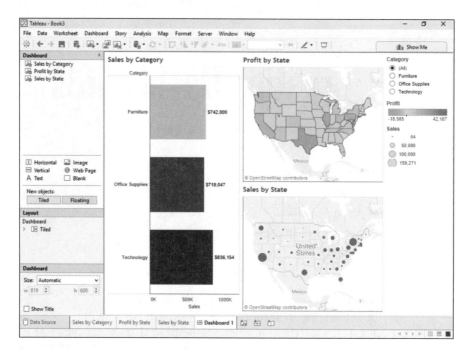

Figure 10-1: Dashboards enable you to tell more of the story in one place.

Dashboards make it easy to see the big picture - providing more of an "executive summary" view.

To prevent nontechnical viewers from being confused when you share your Tableau workbooks, you may want to hide the individual worksheets after you've finished creating your dashboards. Refer to Chapter 9 for more information on hiding and displaying worksheets.

Chapter 11 discusses stories, which offer a more directed approach to leading viewers through your Tableau analyses. Depending on your audience, you may want to use both dashboards and stories in your workbooks.

Adding a Dashboard

Although Tableau workbooks always start out with a new, blank worksheet, you need to actively create any dashboards you want. Fortunately, creating dashboards is quite easy.

To create a new dashboard, follow these steps:

1. **Create the worksheets containing the views that you'll want to use on your dashboard.**

   Although you could begin with a single worksheet, dashboards are generally far more useful when they contain two or more views.

2. **Choose Dashboard ⇨ New Dashboard from Tableau's main menu to create a new, blank dashboard like the one shown in Figure 10-2.**

   Alternatively, you can click the New Dashboard button that appears below the workspace. It's the second button to the right of the worksheet tabs.

3. **Select a worksheet view in the Dashboard panel on the left and drag it onto the dashboard, as shown in Figure 10-3.**

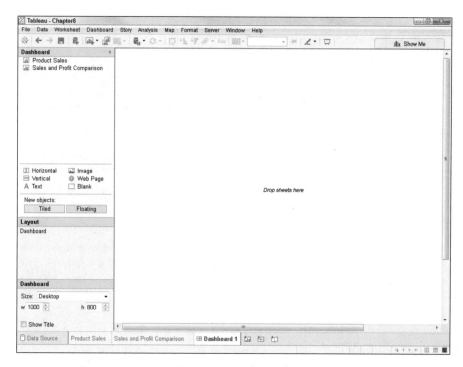

Figure 10-2: Your new dashboard is ready to populate.

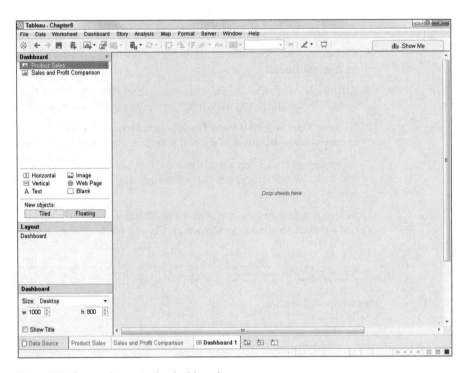

Figure 10-3: Drag a view onto the dashboard.

4. **Release the mouse button to drop the view onto the dashboard.**

   The first view you drop onto the dashboard automatically fills the entire dashboard, as shown in Figure 10-4.

5. **Drag the second view from the Dashboard panel onto the dashboard.**

   As Figure 10-5 shows, Tableau uses a gray box to indicate where the view will appear. Before you drop the second worksheet onto your dashboard, pay attention to this gray placement indicator. Do you want your second sheet to appear above, below, to the right, or to the left of your original sheet?

6. **Release the mouse button when the view is where you want it to appear.**

7. **Continue dragging views onto the dashboard, as shown in Figure 10-6.**

8. **When you've added all the views to the dashboard, select the desired resolution from the Size list box, as shown in Figure 10-7.**

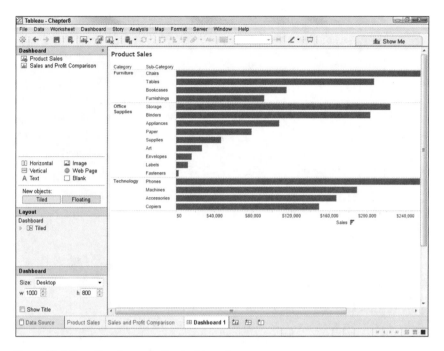

Figure 10-4: Drop the view onto the dashboard.

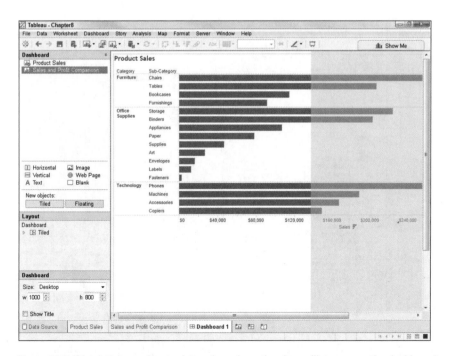

Figure 10-5: Watch the gray box to determine where the view will appear on the dashboard.

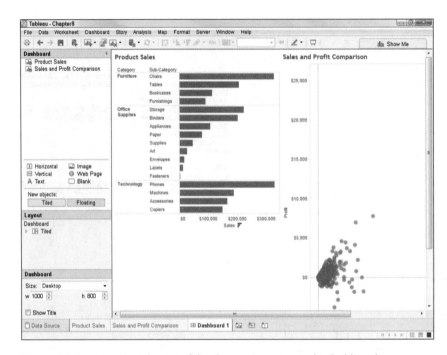

Figure 10-6: Drag and drop the rest of the views you want onto the dashboard.

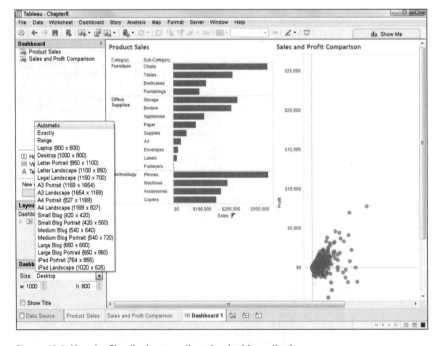

Figure 10-7: Use the Size list box to adjust the dashboard's size.

By default, Tableau tiles any objects that you add to a dashboard so that they don't overlap. If you want more flexibility in the placement of objects, click the Floating button that appears in the New Objects section of the Dashboard panel.

If your individual visualizations don't fit nicely into the container you have provided for them in the dashboard, click on the visualization you want to change and use the drop-down dialogue box in the toolbar to change it to Normal, Fit Width, Fit Height, or Entire View.

Organizing Your Dashboards

Although the dashboard contains the views that you've added, it might not have exactly the appearance that you would like. For example, you might want to add a company logo, adjust the view sizes, or simply move some things around. We take a look at a couple of things that you can do to organize the look and feel of your dashboard.

Adding a logo

Adding a company logo helps give your dashboard the feel of an official company document. If you have access to an image file that contains your logo, you can easily add it to your dashboard as follows:

1. **In the Dashboard panel, below the list of worksheet views, select the Image item and drag it where you'd like the logo to appear on the dashboard, as shown in Figure 10-8.**

   Doing so calls up an Open dialog box.

2. **Using the Open dialog box, navigate to the location of your image file and select it.**

3. **Click the Open button to add the image to the dashboard.**

4. **Right-click the image and choose Fit Image from the contextual menu that appears, as shown in Figure 10-9.**

5. **If necessary, drag the image border to resize the image.**

   Your result should look similar to that shown in Figure 10-10.

Adding a web page

You can also add content from a web page to your dashboard. For example, your company may have a web page that shows the latest company news or allows users to look up products in an online catalog.

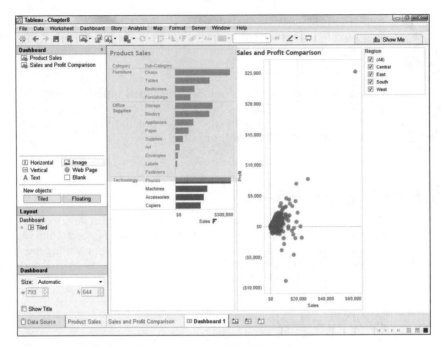

Figure 10-8: Drag the image container onto the dashboard.

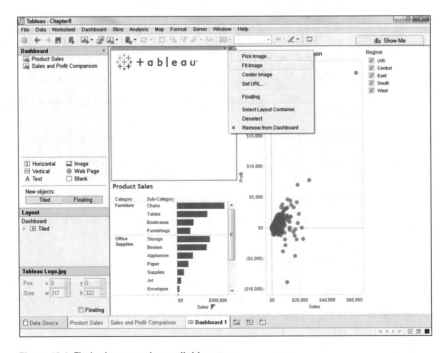

Figure 10-9: Fit the image to the available space.

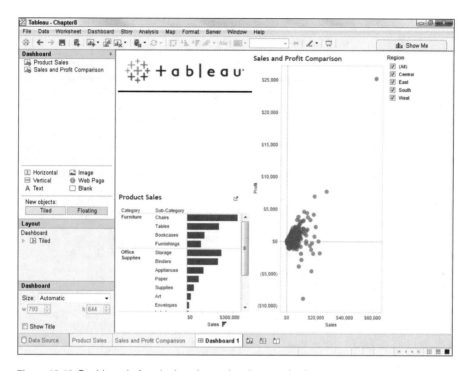

Figure 10-10: Dashboard after the logo image has been resized.

To add a web page to the dashboard, follow these steps:

1. **Drag the Web Page item from the Dashboard panel onto the dashboard, as shown in Figure 10-11.**

2. **In the Edit URL dialog box that appears (see Figure 10-12), enter the URL for the web page that you want to show on the dashboard.**

3. **Click the OK button to add the web page, as shown in Figure 10-13.**

You may want to create a special version of the web page to use on your dashboard to fit the desired content into the available space. Otherwise your users may need to do a lot of scrolling to actually view the content.

Moving and resizing content

After you've added all the content that you want to your dashboard, you'll probably find that the layout of certain elements isn't quite ideal. Fortunately, Tableau gives you the option of moving and also resizing content to fit your needs.

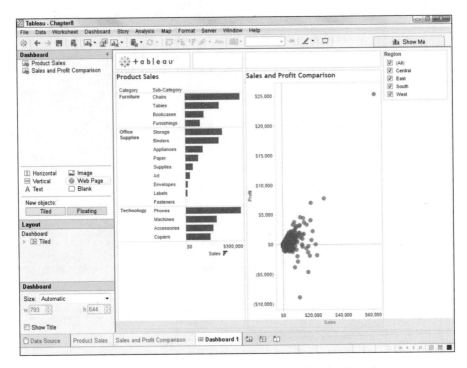

Figure 10-11: Drag the Web Page container onto the bottom of the dashboard.

Figure 10-12: Enter the URL.

Objects on a dashboard sit inside containers that you can move and resize by using the Fit submenu or by dragging its borders. For example, in Figure 10-14, the container for the Product Sales is being adjusted with the help of the Fit submenu.

Figure 10-15 shows how the dashboard appears after several of the items have been moved and resized. You can also add blank objects from the Dashboard panel to help with spacing.

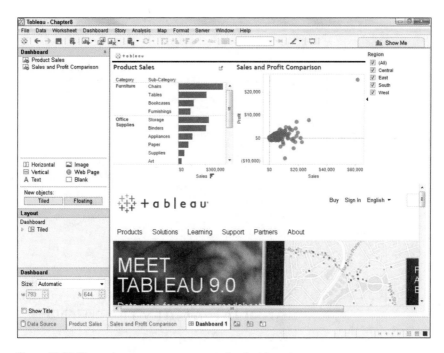

Figure 10-13: The web page now appears on the dashboard.

Figure 10-14: Select a container to resize it.

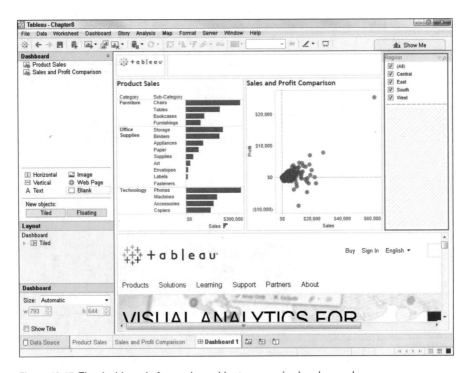

Figure 10-15: The dashboard after various objects are resized and moved.

Ensuring Ease of Use

You want your dashboards to be easy to use whether you only use them yourself or if you share them with other people. In addition to creating an intuitive design for your dashboard, you can do a couple of other things to make your dashboards easier to use. For example, you might want to add a handy quick filter so users can choose what they want to see.

Synchronizing quick filters

When you add a quick filter to a dashboard, you'd probably like it if that filter worked with all the views on the dashboard. That is, when you select something like a Product category using a quick filter, you almost certainly want all the views on that dashboard to reflect your selection.

To synchronize your quick filters across all views on the dashboard, follow these steps:

1. **Right-click the quick filter to display its contextual menu.**

2. **Choose Apply to Worksheets and then select All Using This Data Source, as shown in Figure 10-16.**

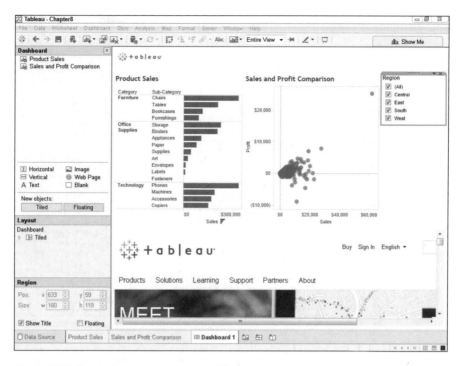

Figure 10-16: Choose how to apply the quick filter.

See Chapter 6 for more information on filtering data in your views.

Hiding the panel

After you've created your dashboard, you don't need to keep the Dashboard panel in view. Not only does the panel use up valuable space, but it's also likely to be confusing for people who share your workbook.

To hide the Dashboard panel, click the double arrows at the right side of the Dashboard Panel title bar. (See Figure 10-17.) Your result should look similar to Figure 10-18.

When the Dashboard panel is hidden, its title bar drops down onto the Tableau status bar in the lower left of the window. If you want to see the Dashboard panel again, click the double arrows in the lower left. (Refer again to Figure 10-18.)

Click to hide the Dashboard panel

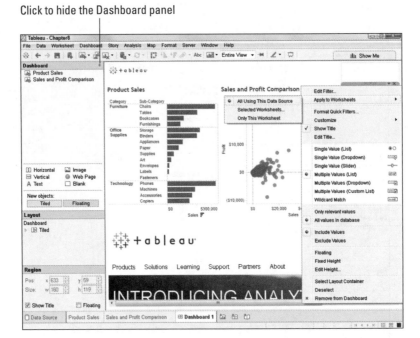

Figure 10-17: Hide the Dashboard panel to make your dashboard easier to use.

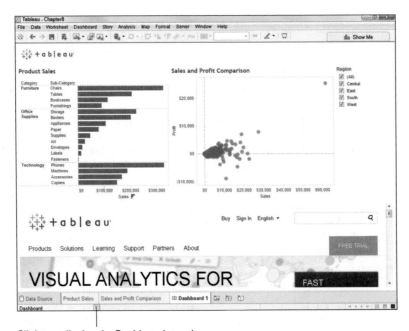

Click to redisplay the Dashboard panel

Figure 10-18: Click the double arrows to once again display the Dashboard panel.

Promoting Exploration through Actions

Actions allow your audience to interact with your visualizations, encouraging them to explore and gain insights. For example, you might include an action that enables users to filter the data on the dashboard by selecting marks within a view.

Using a view as a filter

One of the handiest actions that you can add to a dashboard is to use one of the views as a filter for the other views. That way, users can simply choose one of the marks in that view to see the effects reflected in the other views.

To create an action that uses a view as a filter, follow these steps:

1. **Right-click the view that you want to use as a filter to display its contextual menu, as shown in Figure 10-19.**

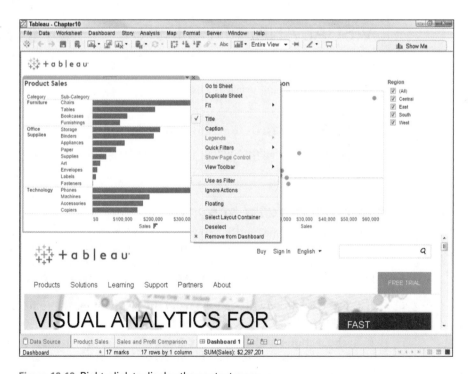

Figure 10-19: Right-click to display the context menu.

2. **Choose the menu's Use as Filter option to create the action.**

3. **Click one of the marks in the view to filter the other views, as shown in Figure 10-20.**

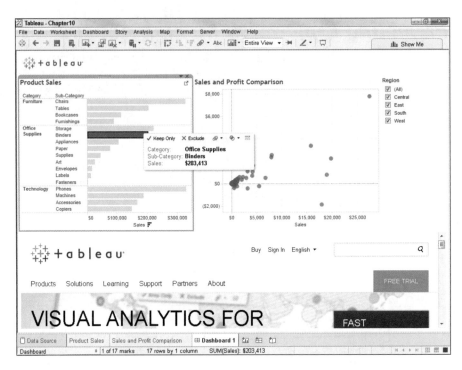

Figure 10-20: Choose a mark to use as a filter.

4. **Click below the axis to remove the filter.**

   You can also click on the mark again to deselect it, or on any space without a mark.

Adding additional actions

You can add additional actions to your dashboard to accomplish other tasks besides filtering the views, such as highlighting targeted information or using URL actions to point to a web page, file, or other web-based resources outside of Tableau. To add additional actions, follow these steps:

1. **Choose Dashboard ⇨ Actions from the Tableau main menu, as shown in Figure 10-21.**

2. **In the Actions dialog box that appears (see Figure 10-22), click the Add Action button to display the types of actions you can add.**

3. **In this case, click the Highlight item to display the Add Highlight Action dialog box shown in Figure 10-23.**

Figure 10-21: Add additional actions to the dashboard.

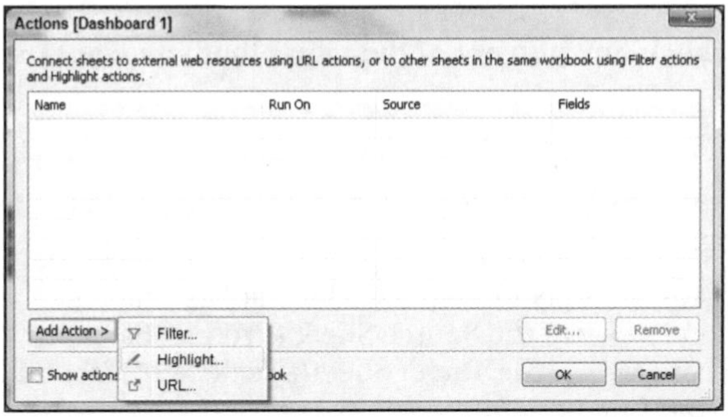

Figure 10-22: Choose the type of action you want to add.

Figure 10-23: Specify the action settings.

4. **Choose how you want to trigger the action by selecting Hover, Select, or Menu.**

   In this case, we will check Select.

5. **Select the check box in front of the views that you want to trigger the action.**

   In this case, we will select them all.

6. **In the Target Highlighting section, specify which fields to target with highlighting.**

   In this case, we will select Category. This implies that when you click on a particular category in the Source Sheet (Product Sales) it will highlight the chosen category in the Target Sheet(s) selected (Product Sales and Sales and Profit Comparison).

7. **Click the OK button to close the Add Highlight Action dialog box.**

8. **Test your action by using the trigger that you selected in Step 4.**

    Figure 10-24 shows the result of the triggering action. In this case, the user clicked on the Category "Technology" in the Souce Sheet (Product Sales), which caused the field(s) targeted (Category value of Technology) to be highlighted in the Target Sheet(s) (Product Sales and Sales and Profit Comparison).

You'll probably need to experiment a bit to get exactly the results that you want. If you need to edit an action, open the Actions dialog box as discussed in Step 1 and then choose Edit.

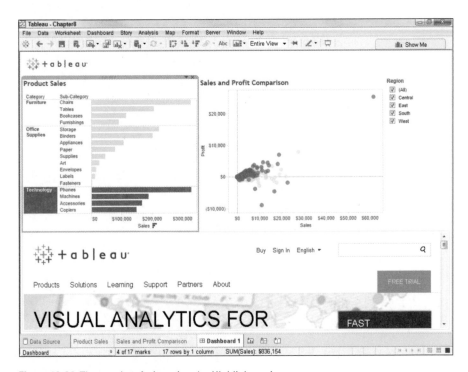

Figure 10-24: The results of triggering the Highlight action.

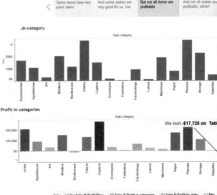

Building Stories

In This Chapter

▶ Seeing what stories can do for you

▶ Bringing purpose to your stories

*A*t times you need to present information in a very structured and directed manner, similar to a PowerPoint presentation. This chapter looks at a Tableau method for creating presentations that lead the viewers along a defined path. That method is the story, and as you'll see, stories can be both useful and powerful.

Discovering the Value of Stories

Tableau is a great tool for creating data analysis and visualizations. Each worksheet you create focuses on a specific analysis, and the dashboards you create enable you to combine several worksheets into an interactive group. Often, workbooks containing worksheets and dashboards are all you need to understand and even share those analyses.

Unfortunately, understanding complex analyses can sometimes be difficult or confusing for people who didn't have a hand in doing the actual analysis. You might be presenting great information, but without a little help, viewers might miss the important points or even misinterpret the information and draw incorrect conclusions.

To get an idea how a Tableau story can help you expose findings for other people, let's take a quick look at a simple story that tells the tale of sales and profits across a range of items for your stores across the country.

Adding a new story in Tableau is as simple as adding a new worksheet or a new dashboard. At the bottom of your screen, click on New Story, just to the right of New Dashboard. Then simply drag the view you want and give it a caption. Continue in this manner until you have built out a story.

Figure 11-1 shows the first story point we want to emphasize: how sales across different sub-categories of products rank against each other. Clearly, certain items like phones and chairs seem to be resulting in quite a bit of sales.

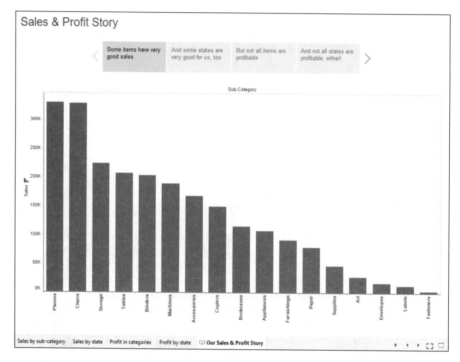

Figure 11-1: Our first story point tells about sales in various subcategories.

Next, our second story point, which you can see in Figure 11-2, shows that a few states, such as California and New York, are enjoying quite good sales. So far, we've given the viewer pretty good news about a few of the items we sell and a few of the places we sell them.

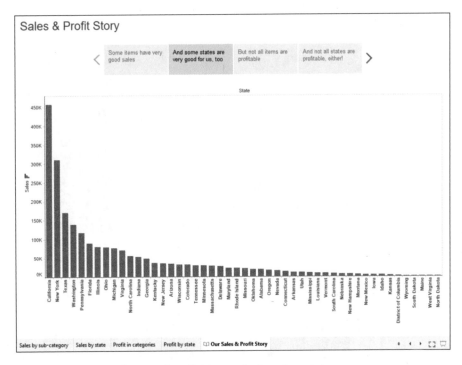

Figure 11-2: Our second story point tells about sales in various states.

Unfortunately, moving onto our third story point shows that we're not making money on everything we sell. In fact, our fourth-highest sales volume item (which happens to be tables) is actually losing money in a fairly substantial way. Figure 11-3 shows this third story point.

Finally, our fourth story point, shown in Figure 11-4, also displays some disturbing news. Texas, the state with our third-highest sales, is also where we're losing the most money.

Even though this story was intentionally kept very simple, it does demonstrate that you can use Tableau stories to guide people through the important points of your analysis. The viewer doesn't need to know anything about using Tableau and he or she certainly doesn't need to be an expert in data analysis.

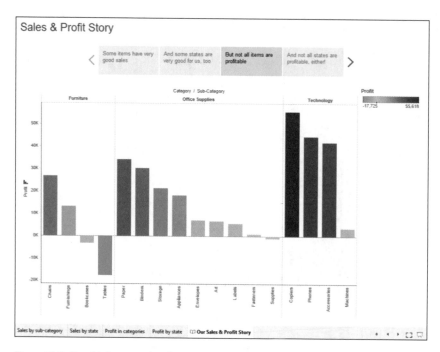

Figure 11-3: Our third story point shows that good sales don't always mean good profits.

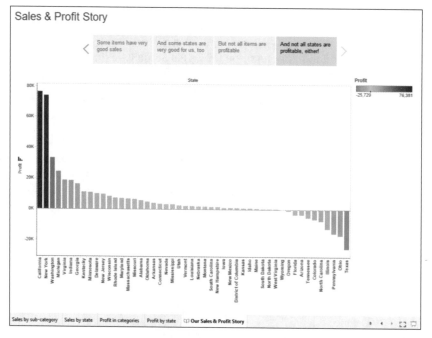

Figure 11-4: Our fourth story point shows that some states aren't very profitable.

Telling Stories with Purpose

The story shown in the first section of this chapter could certainly use some improvements. Tableau gives you a number of ways to make sure that your story serves its purpose. We'll revisit the story by making some changes so that viewers will have an easier time understanding the overall picture.

Figure 11-5 shows a revised version of our first story point. Comparing this story point to the one shown in Figure 11-1, you can see that the subcategories are now sorted alphabetically rather than by the amount of sales.

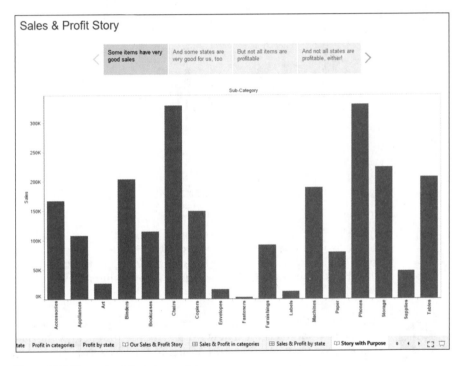

Figure 11-5: The revised first story point.

Next, the second story point was revised as shown in Figure 11-6 to sort the states alphabetically, rather than by the amount of sales. Again, this change was made to make it easier to compare sales and profits.

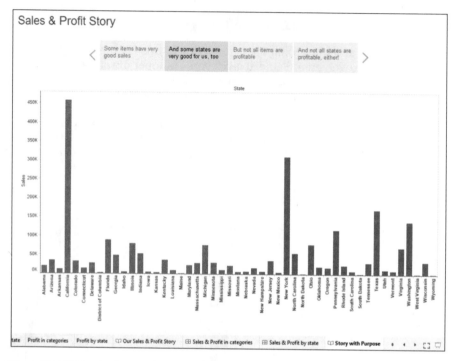

Figure 11-6: The revised second story point.

Figure 11-7 shows the new third story point, which now includes a direct comparison of sales and profits across the subcategories. Also, the lower chart has an annotation added to bring attention to the fact that even though the table sales figures look good, those sales resulted in a pretty big loss of profit.

As an alternative to showing the sales and profits on two separate charts, you might want to create a new worksheet that duplicates the sales by subcategory view and then add profits to the Sales axis.

Finally, Figure 11-8 shows the revision to the fourth story point. In this case, an annotation was added to show that even though Texas seems to have quite good sales, the profit picture there wasn't nearly as rosy as you might like.

Here, too, you could use a single chart that shows both sales and profits by state on the same chart rather than using two charts.

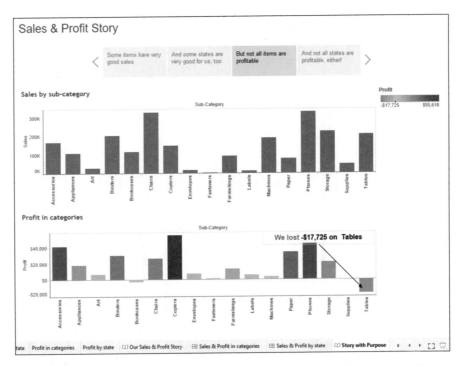

Figure 11-7: The revised third story point now has a direct comparison of sales and profits in the subcategories.

If you're using a story in a live presentation, be sure to click the Presentation Mode button on the toolbar to display the story in full-screen mode. When you're done, press Esc to exit the full-screen mode.

To share your Tableau stories, you can publish to Tableau Server or Tableau Online, or save to Tableau Public. You can also save them in a packaged workbook to send as a file to other Tableau Desktop users or to Tableau Reader users. Chapter 12 and 13 has more information on sharing and publishing.

Actually creating story points in Tableau is easy. You can see an example of creating a Story Point and experience Tableau's free on-demand training at the same time! Go to Tableau's training page http://www.tableau.com/learn/training?qt-training_tabs=1 and navigate to the Story Points video under Dashboards and Stories.

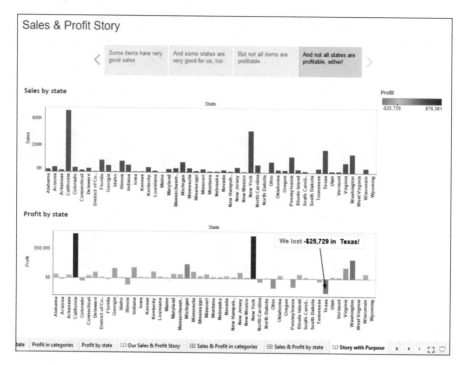

Figure 11-8: The revised fourth story point now has a direct comparison of sales and profits in the states.

Part IV
Publishing and Sharing

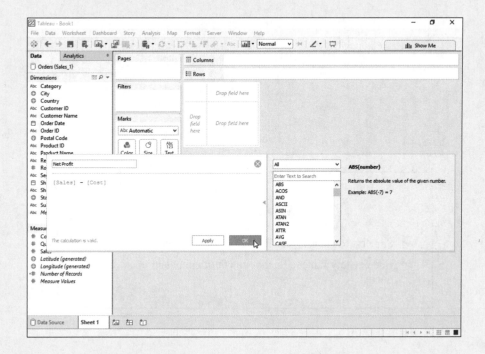

For more on collaborating with Tableau, see www.dummies.com/extras/
tableau.

In this part . . .

- See how to publish your Tableau workbooks online.
- Find out how Tableau Reader can fill your collaboration needs.

Publishing Workbooks

In This Chapter

▶ Getting to know Tableau publishing options

▶ Serving up your workbooks

▶ Sharing nicely

*Y*ou almost certainly want to share your Tableau workbooks with other people. *Publishing* is the term that Tableau uses for making your workbooks available to other users. This chapter looks at the publishing options that you can use.

Understanding Publishing

Publishing means saving your Tableau workbooks in a location where other people can access them in a browser. You can share your workbooks to a server on your local network with Tableau Server. Or, you can publish them to the cloud with Tableau Online, so they can be accessed with proper authorization through the Internet. You can also share your workbooks to Tableau Public, which will make them publicly available on the Internet.

Tableau also has a product called Tableau Online. In the context of this chapter, when we use "online" we refer to sharing the workbooks in a central location. When referring to the Tableau-hosted product, we will say "Tableau Online."

Depending on the version of Tableau Desktop you're using, you may not have all three publishing options available. Tableau Professional Edition supports all three, but Tableau Personal Edition can only publish to Tableau Public and create packaged workbooks/PDFs/images. Tableau Desktop Public Edition cannot save any local files and can only publish to Tableau Public.

Tableau Public and Tableau Online are both ways to publish your content to the Internet. The difference is that Tableau Public is for sharing your views with the world! Tableau Online provides you with the same security and control that you would expect from any cloud-based enterprise software provider. Tableau Online and Tableau Server are both ways that you can share Tableau dashboards and views securely with other users in your company. Both require a logon, a license, and security credentials. The difference is that with Tableau Server, you install the Tableau Server software and support it yourself. With Tableau Online, Tableau does all that work for you, as the server is hosted in the cloud.

Because Tableau Public stores your workbooks on the Internet without any security, you'll probably want to be careful about publishing any workbooks that contain sensitive or proprietary information.

Tableau Server needs at least 15GB of free disk space to install. In addition, if you have a 64-bit system, you'll need at least a four-core processor and 8GB of RAM. (32-bit systems can get by with two-core processors and 4GB of RAM.) Most modern computers should easily meet these requirements, but you might run into problems if you want to install Tableau Server on a virtual machine that isn't configured to meet these minimums. The installation program simply won't run if it doesn't detect a system that meets the minimum requirements.

Sharing Your Tableau Workbooks

Publishing your Tableau workbooks so that others can view and interact with them is a fairly straightforward process. For the following example, we'll use Tableau Online, but if you use Tableau Server or Tableau Public, you'll find the steps are quite similar.

Both Tableau Server and Tableau Online require that you be a licensed user. If you don't have access to these environments, you can still try out the interface by sharing your content on Tableau Public. Just make sure it is information you don't mind sharing with the world!

If you want to publish to Tableau Public, you will still need to register to create an account, but the account is free.

To publish a Tableau workbook to Tableau Online, follow these steps:

1. **With your workbook complete, choose Server ⇨ Publish Workbook from Tableau's main menu, as shown in Figure 12-1.**

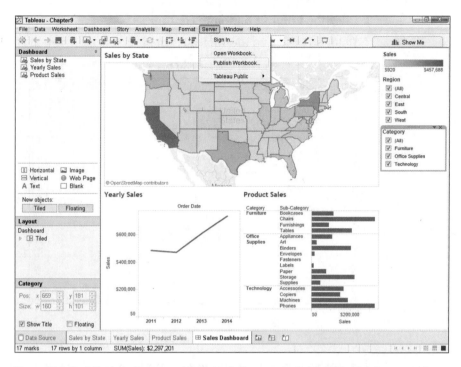

Figure 12-1: Both Tableau Server and Tableau Online use the Publish Workbook command.

2. **In the Sign In dialog box that appears, enter the required server address.**

   As Figure 12-2 shows, the required address for Tableau Online is `https://online.tableau.com`. If you are using Tableau Server, you'll need to enter the correct network address for your server. If you don't know the address, ask your network or Tableau Server administrator.

Figure 12-2: Enter the proper server address.

3. Click the Connect button to continue.

Doing so brings up the Tableau Sign In screen, as shown in Figure 12-3.

Figure 12-3: The Tableau Sign In screen.

4. Enter your username in the screen's Email field and then click Sign In.

The screen refreshes to display a Password field, as shown in Figure 12-4.

For Tableau Online, your username will always be your email address.

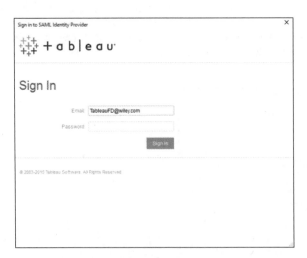

Figure 12-4: The Password field.

5. Enter your password, and then click the Sign In button to continue.

As Figure 12-5 shows, Tableau Online brings up a screen informing you that it doesn't allow external database connections, so you'll need to create a data extract. If you've already created your data extract, you can jump forward to Step 10.

Figure 12-5: You need to create a data extract for Tableau Online when using flat files or non-cloud-based data sources (like SQL Server).

6. Click the screen's Create Data Extract link to open the Extract Data dialog box, shown in Figure 12-6.

Figure 12-6: Specify any filters or other options for the data extract.

7. **After specifying any filters or other options for the data extract, click the Extract button to display the Save Extract As dialog box shown in Figure 12-7.**

   For more on creating data extracts, see Chapter 4.

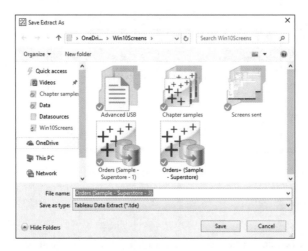

Figure 12-7: You can use the default location for saving the data extract.

8. **Click the Save button to continue.**

9. **After the data extract is saved, select Server⇨ Publish Workbook from Tableau's main menu.**

   Doing so displays the Publish Workbook dialog box, as shown in Figure 12-8. Here you can choose things such as who can view the workbook and which sheets they can see.

10. **After you've selected any options you want, click the Publish button to display the preview, as shown in Figure 12-9.**

You can control who can access your workbook during the Publish process, using the View Permissions menu shown in Figure 12-8, later in the chapter. You can also change those permissions after you've published the workbook. The next section describes how.

Figure 12-8: Choose any options you want before publishing the workbook.

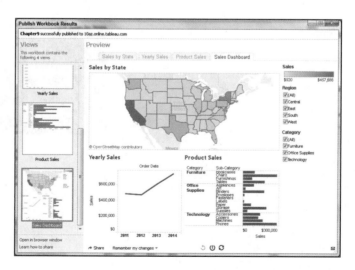

Figure 12-9: Tableau provides a preview of your published workbook.

Providing Access to Analysis

After you've published your workbooks to Tableau Server or Tableau Online, you can edit who can access them. (This is not possible with Tableau Public, however.) In addition, you also have the option to choose how users can interact with the published workbooks.

To control access, follow these steps:

1. **In the Workbook Preview screen, shown back in Figure 12-9, click the Open in Browser Window link in the screen's lower-left corner.**

   If you've already closed that window, you can also open your web browser and enter `https://sso.online.tableau.com/public/prelogin`. Either way, you'll open the Sign In screen, as shown in Figure 12-10.

Figure 12-10: You need to sign in.

2. **Enter your email address and click the Sign In button to display the Password box, as shown in Figure 12-11.**

Figure 12-11: The Password box.

3. **Enter your password, and then click the Sign In button to display the published workbook, as shown in Figure 12-12.**

4. **Click the Permissions tab to display the screen shown in Figure 12-13.**

5. **Use the options on this screen to control what users can do with the published workbook.**

To set permissions for specific users, add a new user and then set the specific permissions that you want that user to have.

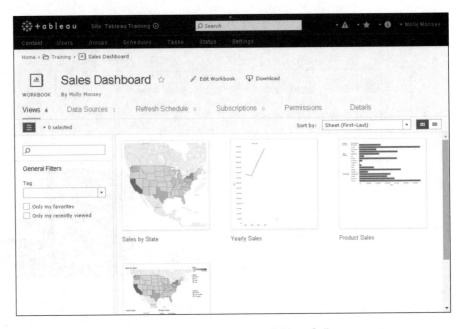

Figure 12-12: Your published workbook as it appears on Tableau Online.

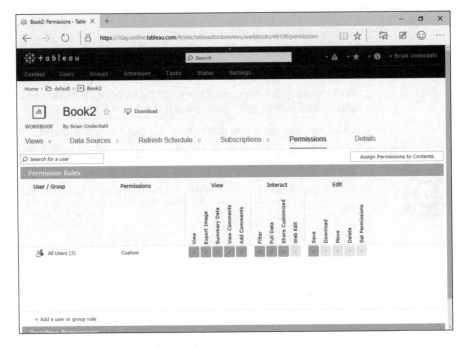

Figure 12-13: Use this screen to control access.

13

Sharing Files with Tableau Reader

. . . .

In This Chapter

▶ Seeing how you can share your work with people who don't have Tableau

▶ Making sure that people can see what you've shared

. . . .

Tableau Reader is a free desktop application you can use to interact with data visualizations built in Tableau Desktop. With Tableau Reader, you can filter, drill down, and view data details as designed by the author without needing to have a full copy of Tableau Desktop installed.

Looking at the Reader App

Let's face it: Tableau is a very powerful tool for doing data analyses and visualizations. But there may be times when you want to share your amazing work with somebody who is not a licensed Tableau Desktop user and none of the publishing options are available to you. They simply need a way to open and view Tableau workbooks with abilities to interact. The Tableau Reader app is a simple and free way for them to do this.

To download and install Tableau Reader, follow these steps:

1. **Open your web browser and navigate to** `http://tableau.com/products/reader`, **as shown in Figure 13-1.**

2. **Click the Download Reader Now button to begin the download.**

   A new page appears, displaying the progress of your download, as shown in Figure 13-2.

Figure 13-1: Users can download Tableau Reader for free.

3. **When the download is finished, click the Run button in the prompt box at the bottom of the screen, as shown in Figure 13-3.**

4. **In the new dialog box that appears, click the View License Agreement button, read the agreement when it appears, and then select the check box to indicate your agreement, as shown in Figure 13-4.**

5. **Click the dialog box's Install button and wait for the installation to complete.**

   Depending on your system settings, you may need to indicate that you want to allow the program to make changes to your system.

   When the installation finishes, you'll see an Activate Tableau Reader dialog box prompting you to provide registration information.

6. **Enter the required registration information, as shown in Figure 13-5.**

7. **Click the dialog box's Register button to continue.**

   If your registration is correct, you'll see a Registration Completed notice, as shown in Figure 13-6.

8. **Click the Continue button to open Tableau Reader.**

Figure 13-2: Wait a few moments for the download to complete.

Figure 13-3: After the download completes, click Run to begin the installation.

Figure 13-4: You must agree to the license agreement to complete the installation.

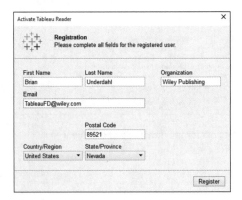

Figure 13-5: Complete the registration information.

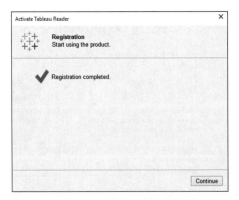

Figure 13-6: Your registration is complete.

Providing Access

Tableau Reader can only open Tableau-packaged workbooks. *Packaged workbooks* are Tableau workbooks that can contain the data within them. To include the data, you need to use a file-based source like Excel or CSV, or you will need to extract your data from the source using Tableau Data Extracts. Fortunately, it's very easy for you to produce these workbooks for distribution.

Tableau Reader does not offer the same level of security as Tableau Online or Tableau Server, which require a user to input credentials. Tableau packaged workbooks can be forwarded and viewed by anyone. If your workbook contains sensitive information, you'll probably want to share it using Tableau Server or Tableau Online.

To prepare your Tableau workbooks so that they can be opened in Tableau Reader, follow these steps:

1. **With the workbook you want to prepare open, choose File ⇨ Export Packaged Workbook from the Tableau main menu, as shown in Figure 13-7.**

Figure 13-7: Export your workbook as a packaged workbook for use in Tableau Reader.

2. **Using the Export Packaged Workbook dialog box that appears, navigate to the location where you want to save the packaged workbook and make sure that you provide a descriptive name in the File Name field, as shown in Figure 13-8.**

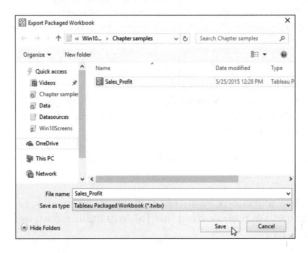

Figure 13-8: Use a descriptive name so that users will know the purpose of the workbook.

3. **Click the Save button to save your workbook.**

You can save the packaged workbook in a location that users can access on your network, or you can send it to them as a file attachment to an email message.

Opening packaged workbooks in Tableau Reader is simple, but we'll review the process so that you can tell your users what they need to know when they call for help. Follow these steps:

1. **Open the Tableau Reader to display the Start page, as shown in Figure 13-9.**

2. **In the Open section in the center of the window, click the Open a Workbook link to display the Open dialog box, as shown in Figure 13-10.**

3. **Using the Open dialog box, navigate to the location where the packaged workbook is saved and then select the correct packaged workbook.**

4. **Click the Open button to open the workbook, as shown in Figure 13-11.**

Tableau Reader users will be able to view and interact with your worksheets, dashboards, and stories, but they won't be able to modify your workbooks.

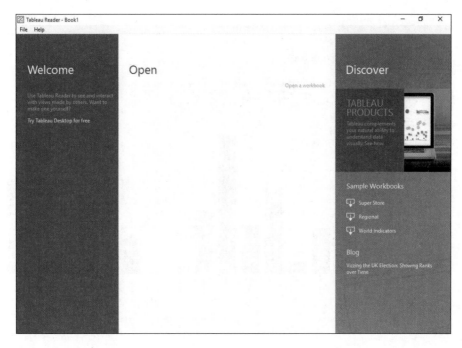

Figure 13-9: The Tableau Reader Start page.

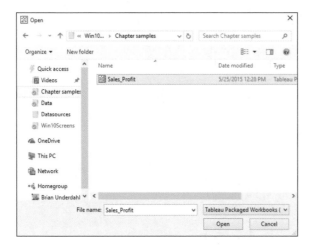

Figure 13-10: Choose the packaged workbook to open.

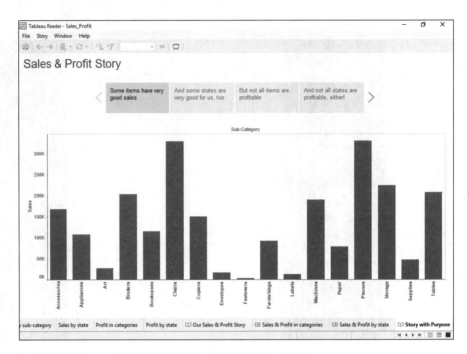

Figure 13-11: The packaged workbook is open in Tableau Reader.

Part V
Advancing to a Higher Level

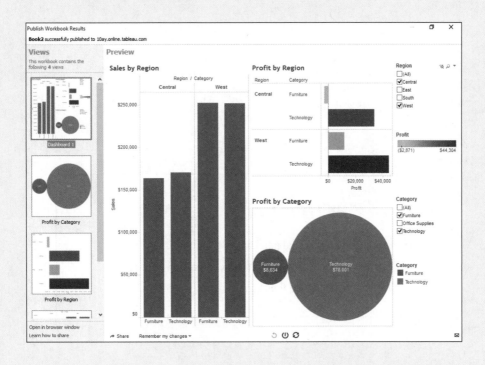

For more on keeping your Tableau Desktop secure and running efficiently, see www.dummies.com/extras/tableau.

In this part . . .

- Learn advanced visual analytics techniques.
- Find out how to add your own calculations to worksheets.
- Work with calculated fields.

Forecast

Add a
Forecast

Forecast

Add a
Forecast

14

Forecast

Add a
Forecast

Forecast

Add a
Forecast

Fore

Advanced Visual Analytics

- -

In This Chapter

▶ Getting more from your analyses

▶ Asking deeper questions

- -

*Y*ou can do an awful lot in Tableau simply by dragging and dropping fields in the workspace. But if you give yourself a chance to explore further, you'll see additional power from Tableau. This chapter gives you the opportunity to take your data analyses and visualizations up a notch by introducing some of the more advanced data analysis options that you'll find in Tableau.

Using Advanced Analytics

Advanced analytics is a rather broad term we'll use to encompass a number of different things that you can do in Tableau. As you'll see in the following sections, each advanced analytics technique provides powerful methods that enable you to understand your data in completely new ways.

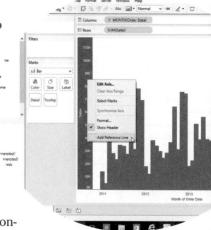

Calculations

Calculations are operations (usually mathematical) that enable you to manipulate the data contained in your data sources to produce useful new values for your data analyses. A prime example of a calculation would be determining your profit by subtracting costs from the selling price of items. Data sources generally contain the raw data in fields such as cost and sales, but calculated amounts like profit usually aren't stored in the database because doing so is inefficient. Any value that's easily calculated from existing database fields would be a waste of data storage space, so database designers intentionally exclude such values from the database definition.

If you've used a spreadsheet, you know that many types of calculations are possible that go well beyond simply determining the difference between two values. In fact, the subject of calculations is so important in Tableau that we're going to give calculations their own chapters rather than trying to cover them here. See Chapters 15 and 16 for a lot more information on calculations in Tableau.

Parameters

You can use *parameters* in calculations instead of using constant values. For example, you could use a parameter to specify the sales goal for a reference line rather than specifying one value. By using a parameter, you can make it easy to select different values based on what's needed in your analysis rather than having the analysis locked into a specific condition.

Parameters are covered in more detail in Chapter 15.

Totals

Often when creating a visualization, you may discover that you want to add totals and sub-totals to your view. (You may have selected a chart type that shows a table with values, for example.) With Tableau, it is simple to include both sub-totals and grand totals for measures.

To add totals, follow these steps:

1. **Drag fields to shelves as shown in Figure 14-1 to create the table displayed.**

2. **Choose Analysis⇨Totals from the Tableau main menu and then select either the Show Row Grand Totals or the Show Column Grand Totals option, depending on which totals you want to include, as shown in Figure 14-2.**

   When you make your selection, Tableau adds the appropriate totals to the view, as shown in Figure 14-3. (In this case, Row Grand Totals was selected.)

3. **To add Column Grand Totals, return to Step 2 and choose Add Column Grand Totals from the Totals submenu. To add sub-totals, return to Step 2 and choose the Add All Sub-totals option from the same submenu.**

   Doing so yields the results shown in Figure 14-4.

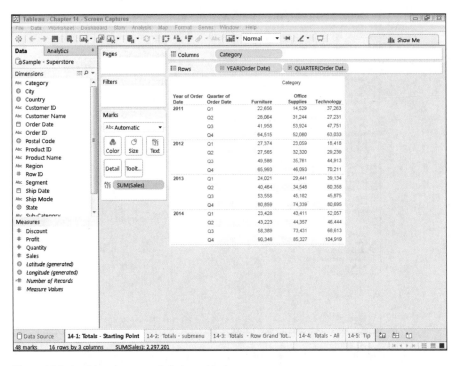

Figure 14-1: A table prior to totals being added.

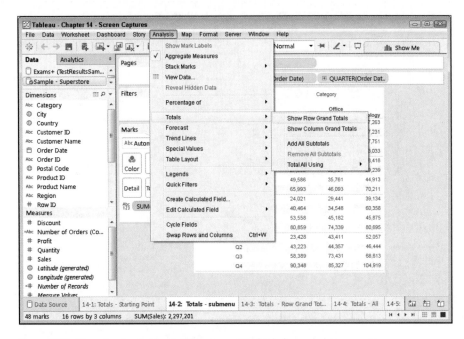

Figure 14-2: Choosing the type of totals you want to include.

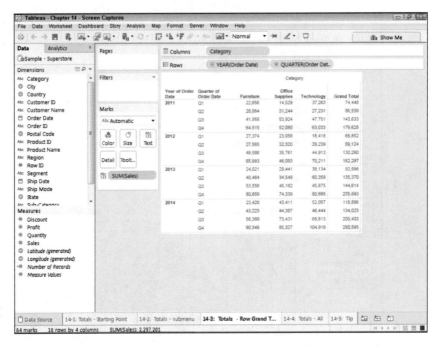

Figure 14-3: Seeing the results.

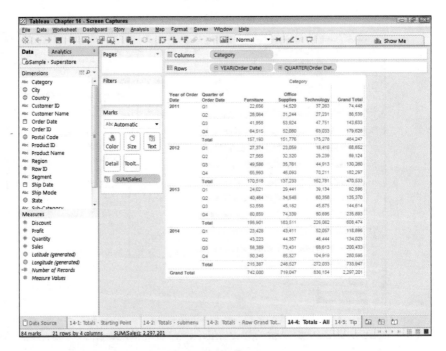

Figure 14-4: Choosing Grand Totals and All Sub-Totals.

TIP

If multiple levels of sub-totals in your visualization are just a bit much, just right-click a field and uncheck Sub-totals in the contextual menu that appears. Figure 14-5 shows us working with Sub-totals for the Quarter(Order Date) field.

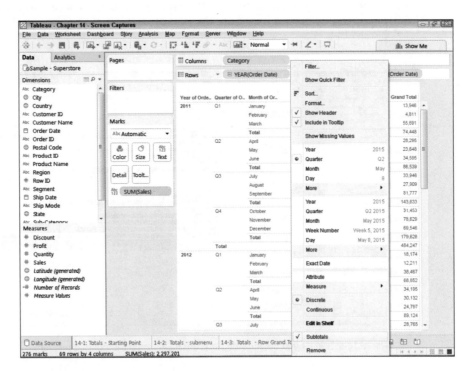

Figure 14-5: Manually removing a level of sub-totals.

Reference lines, bands, distributions, and boxes

Another way to enhance your Tableau visualizations is by adding a reference line, band, distribution, or box plot to the chart. This feature is useful for indicating things such as average sales, product sales goals, and so on. For example, you could use a reference line to indicate the minimum sales target so that it will be easy to see which stores have achieved their goal and which stores have fallen short.

Tableau gives you considerable latitude in adding reference lines, bands, distributions, or box plots. We look at each of these individually in the following sections.

Reference lines

Reference lines are straight lines that originate from a constant or computed value on an axis.

To add a reference line, click on the Analytics tab and choose add reference. Add Reference Line from the pop-up menu that appears, as shown in Figure 14-6.

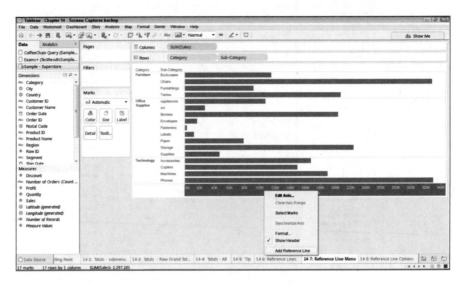

Figure 14-6: Begin by choosing Add Reference Line from the contextual menu.

Figure 14-7 shows the options that appear in the dialog box for reference lines.

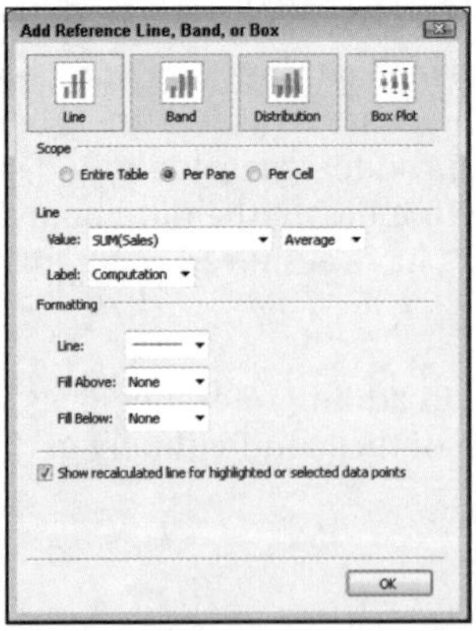

Figure 14-7: The Reference Line options.

First, using the options under the Scope heading, choose whether you want the reference line to be the same across the entire view or whether you want it to be different for each pane or each cell in the chart. (Figure 14-8 shows examples of each.)

The Per Cell option is often used to compare an actual value to a target value, while Entire Table and Per Pane might be used to compare bars to an average.

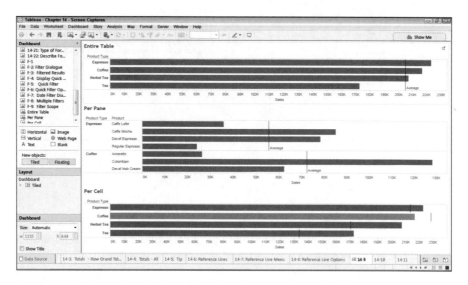

Figure 14-8: Understanding the Entire Table, Per Pane, and Per Cell options.

Reference lines will recalculate and dynamically change based on selections you make in the view. Simply click on a few marks and, while the original reference line stays intact, it fades, and an updated reference line will appear until you clear or change your selections.

Next, you need to specify the line settings by choosing the measure or value that will be the basis for your reference line. You can also select the appropriate aggregation or value as Average, Constant, Maximum, Median, Minimum, Sum, or Total. For example, if you wanted your reference line to appear at a specific number representing a sales goal, you would choose Constant and then specify the value or choose a field from your data set that contains those target values.

You can then choose how to label and format the line. There are several choices for labels, but notice that the default is set as Computation (such as Average, Maximum, and so on).

In this case, choose to show a reference line for Average Sum(Sales) for each pane, as shown in Figure 14-9.

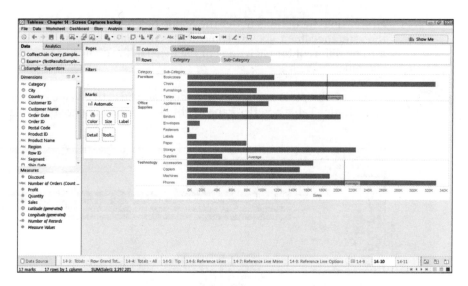

Figure 14-9: Choosing Average Sum(Sales) for each pane.

Reference bands

Reference bands are shaded areas behind the marks in the view between two constant or computed values on the axis. You can add reference bands to any continuous axis.

Distributions

Distributions are similar to reference bands, except with options for gradient shading to indicate the distribution of values along an axis. Figure 14-10 shows an example of a reference distribution that shows monthly sales over time as well as how those values are distributed.

For distributions, you can choose Confidence Interval, Percentages, Percentiles, Quantiles, or Standard Deviation. In addition, you can choose the formatting for the gradient.

Box plots

Box plots, also known as box-and-whisker plots, are a visually concise way of seeing and contrasting distributions of data. The boxes show the middle 50% of the data (or in other words, the middle two quartiles of data). Whiskers are added to box plots to show further information about the distribution of the data. In Tableau Desktop, whiskers can be configured to show either the full extent of the data or 1.5 times the interquartile range (the length of the box). Use the latter to help identify potential outliers.

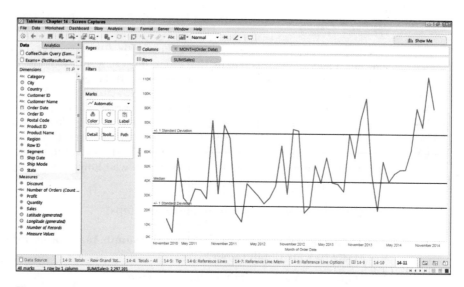

Figure 14-10: An example of a reference distribution.

Normally when creating a box plot you are showing the distribution of values across different dimensions. Thus, you will want to be sure to disaggregate the data with one of two options. You can add one or more dimensions to Detail on the Marks card or you can uncheck Aggregate Measures, as shown in Figure 14-11.

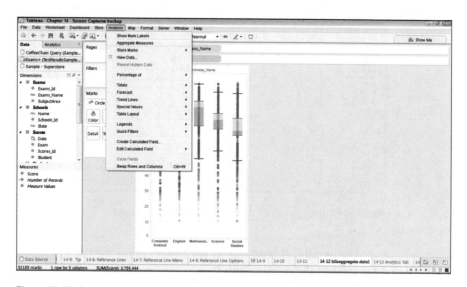

Figure 14-11: A sample box plot where you are disaggregating the data.

Trend lines

Trend lines display data trends using lines of best fit based on statistical models. Essentially, this means that trend lines use your existing data to help determine whether results can be accurately predicted.

With trend lines, you can answer questions such as whether profit is predicted by sales or if average delays at an airport are significantly correlated with the month of the year. Trend lines use statistical models to help you determine whether the value of one variable helps you predict the value of another. For example, would you expect to wait longer at the airport in December than you would in October?

To add trend lines to the view, follow these steps:

1. **Add Sales to your Rows shelf and the Month Year option for Order Date to your Columns shelf.**

2. **Open the Analytics tab of the Data pane.**

3. **Drag the Trend Line option from the pane onto the view, as shown in Figure 14-12.**

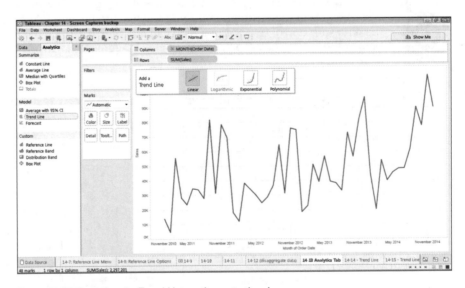

Figure 14-12: Dragging the Trend Line option onto the view.

4. **Optionally, choose one of the model types for the line before you release the mouse button.**

   Figure 14-13 shows the result of selecting the Linear model.

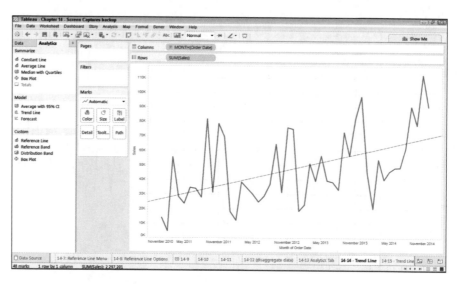

Figure 14-13: Tableau displays the trend line.

5. **To modify a trend line, right-click the trend line and choose Edit Trend Lines from the menu that appears.**

    Doing so brings up the Trend Lines Options dialog box, as shown in Figure 14-14.

6. **Using the Trend Lines Options dialog box, make any modifications that you want and then click OK.**

    You can view the actual formula that's used to calculate the trend line by hovering your mouse pointer over the line, as shown in Figure 14-15.

Figure 14-14: Your Trend Lines options.

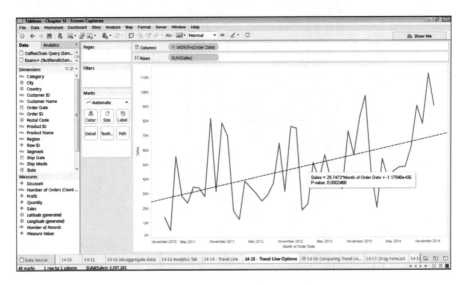

Figure 14-15: Tableau displays the calculation used to create the trend line.

Forecasting

Forecasting is a means of predicting what will happen in the future based on historical data. Even though forecasting can be, to some extent, guesswork, most businesses use forecasting to help predict where the market will head.

In Tableau, forecasts are based on sophisticated models that look at the trends in the past to help predict future results. Tableau uses a technique known as *exponential smoothing* where recent results have more weight than older results.

When preparing a forecast, Tableau compares the results of up to eight different forecasting models to see which produces the highest quality results. Don't worry though; Tableau will make the best selection based on your data in the view, but the forecasts can always be edited. The methods used are discussed in detail in the Tableau help.

Forecasting projects results using time series data, so keep in mind that you can only use forecasting in Tableau if your analysis includes a date and at least one measure. There are scenarios that will not allow for forecasting, such as when using disaggregated data, totals, and table calculations.

To see how forecasting works in Tableau, let's create a simple example:

1. **Open a new workbook using a data source that contains both date values and numeric values.**

   For this example, the Tableau Superstore sample is a good choice.

2. **Drag the Sales Measure onto the Rows shelf.**

3. **Drag the Order Date dimension onto the Columns shelf.**

4. **Click the down arrow at the right side of the Order Date dimension on the Columns shelf to display the context menu and choose a continuous date option.**

   In this case, choose the option to display the continuous month, shown as Month May 2015.

5. **Click the Analytics tab in the Data pane to display the analytics options.**

6. **Select Forecast and drag it onto the view, as shown in Figure 14-16.**

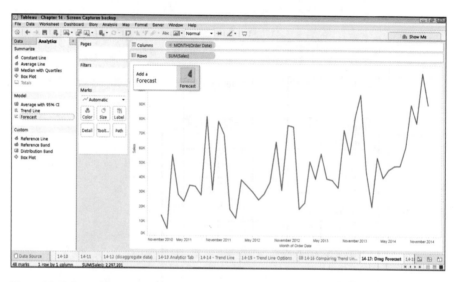

Figure 14-16: Dragging Forecast onto the view.

7. **Examine the chart, as shown in Figure 14-17, to see how the sales are forecast to continue based upon the existing data.**

8. **Choose Analysis ➪ Forecast ➪ Forecast Options from the Tableau main menu.**

   Doing so calls up the Forecast Options dialog box, as shown in Figure 14-18.

9. **Using the dialog box, choose any options you want to use to modify the forecast.**

   For example, you could use the options in the Forecast Length section to create a longer-term forecast.

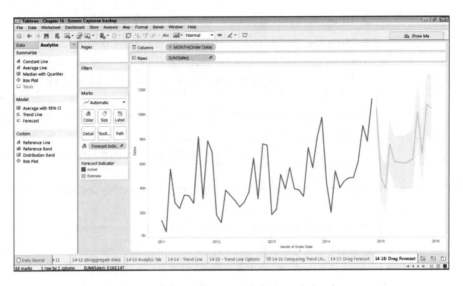

Figure 14-17: The sales forecast is based upon trends in the existing data.

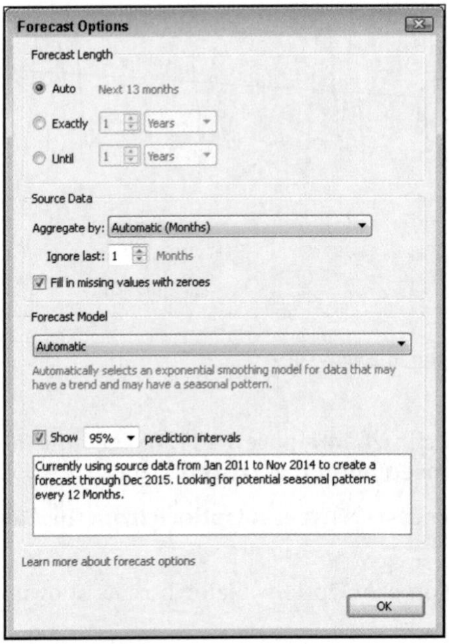

Figure 14-18: Choosing the options you want to modify the forecast.

When Tableau creates a forecast, it is not sure of when the last time period has completed. As a result, it defaults to throwing away the measure value from the last time period, which in this case is December 2014. In our scenario, we will assume that the year is complete, so we want to include December in our Actual Data and begin our forecast in January 2015. In order to do that, just choose 0 Months in the Ignore Last . . . Months drop-down menu in the Forecast Options dialog box. Your forecast will now begin in January 2015, as shown in Figure 14-19.

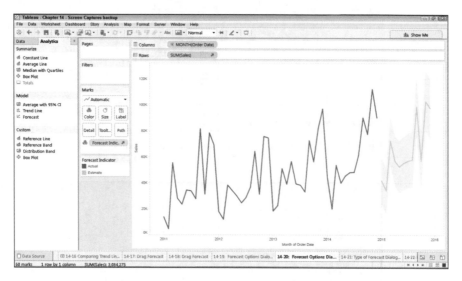

Figure 14-19: Changing Forecast Options to begin forecast in January 2015.

Forecasts are exactly that — forecasts, not assurances. Choosing a forecast length that's too long can greatly increase the probability that the forecast will contain large errors.

To see additional information about how the forecast was created, right-click the view and choose Forecast ⇨ Describe Forecast from the contextual menu that appears, as shown in Figure 14-20. Doing so displays the Describe Forecast dialog box, as shown in Figure 14-21.

You can't change any of the information in the Describe Forecast dialog box, but if you want to save the information for documentation purposes, click the Copy to Clipboard button. You'll then be able to paste that information into another document.

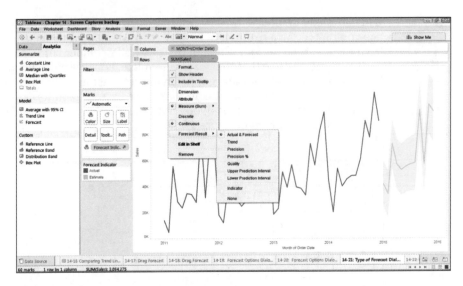

Figure 14-20: Choosing the type of forecast result to display.

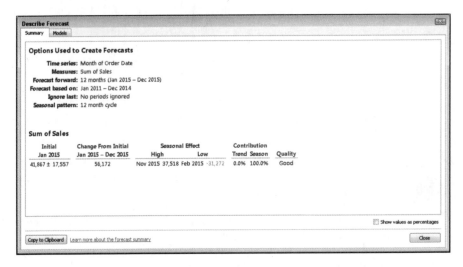

Figure 14-21: Viewing additional information about the forecast.

Creating Calculations

In This Chapter

▶ Understanding the value of calculations
▶ Creating different types of calculations
▶ Customizing data with parameters

*A*t times, raw data simply isn't sufficient for what you might need. Tableau gives you the option to expand your analysis by building calculations based off of the raw data. This chapter discusses ways that you'll find calculations useful, and also shows you how to perform calculations in Tableau.

Seeing How Calculations Can Be Useful

If you have experience using databases, you're probably aware that in most cases, those databases are designed to hold only as much information as is needed. Often, information that can be derived from the database using calculations isn't stored. An example that's commonly cited is the line total of a sale. Often the sales price and quantity sold are stored, but the total is not because it can be calculated by multiplying the first two.

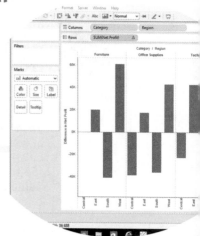

The following sections take a look at some of the ways that you can use calculations in Tableau.

Calculated fields

Calculated fields are fields that you create that don't already exist in your data source. These calculated fields are created using formulas that are often based on other fields. For example, Figure 15-1 shows a calculated field called Profit Ratio, which uses the formula SUM([Profit]) / SUM([Sales]). After you've created this calculated field, you can use it in your views or in other calculations just like any existing field in the data source.

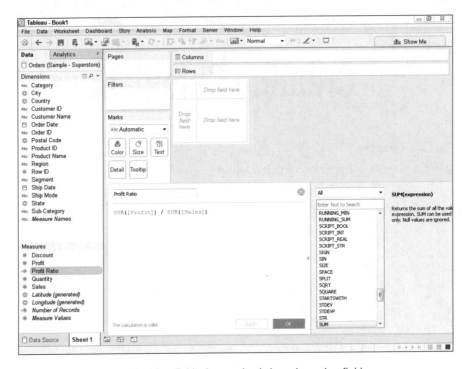

Figure 15-1: A calculated field is a field whose value is based on other fields.

Notice in Figure 15-1 that field names used in formulas are enclosed in square brackets. Technically, Tableau only requires the brackets for field names that contain spaces, but it's a good practice in any event because if you forget to include them when they are needed, you'll have an error that's hard to find.

Table calculations

Table calculations are applied to values that come back from the database at some aggregation level. It's akin to building a pivot table and running calculations on it afterwards. Table calculations rely on the detail (and often the structure) of the view. As Figure 15-2 shows, you can use Tableau's Table Calculation options to show things such as running totals, rankings, or even growth. Table calculations frequently calculate values across two or more rows. For example, a table calculation could figure out how much this month's sales compare to last month's sales in cases where your result set returns a row for each month.

Tableau marks table calculations by placing a triangle mark at the right side of the field, indicating that a change has been made.

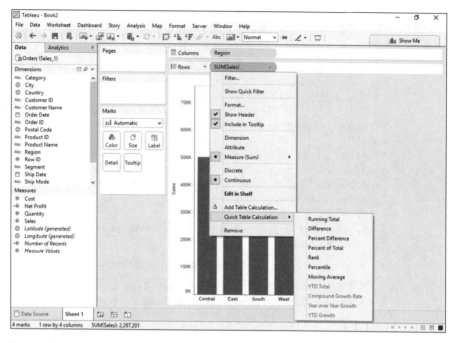

Figure 15-2: Table calculations apply across the table.

Creating Calculations and Parameters

You've seen that calculations can be very useful in Tableau. In the following sections, we dig into the nuts and bolts of actually creating calculations. In addition, we'll have a look at *parameters,* which provide a handy way of dynamically changing values that are used in calculations, filters, and reference lines.

Creating calculated fields

You create calculated fields in Tableau using formulas. You can include the following elements in a formula:

- ✔ **Fields:** These consist of the existing fields in your data source and can include other calculated fields and sets. In formulas, fields appear in orange text.

- ✔ **Functions:** These are built-in operations that can be performed on data, such as COUNT, DATETIME, SUM, FIND, and DAY. Functions appear as light blue text in formulas.

- ✔ **Operators:** These include the standard mathematical operators like +, –, and *. Operators show up as black text in formulas.

✔ **Parameters:** These are placeholder variables that you can use in a formula so that the actual value is specified at runtime. Parameters appear as purple text in formulas.

✔ **Comments:** You can add comments to your formulas to provide a level of documentation. Comments show up as green text in formulas. Items you enter after two forward slash marks are considered comments.

Chapter 16 provides more information about Tableau's built-in functions.

You can create quite complex calculated fields, but for this example, we'll have a look at creating something simple — a Profit Ratio field that's the result of dividing the sum of the profit measure by the sum of the sales measure. Here's what you need to do:

1. **After you've connected to your data source in Tableau, open a worksheet.**

    You can use an existing worksheet or a new worksheet.

2. **Click the down arrow to the right of the Dimensions header and choose Create Calculated Field from the pop-up menu that appears, as shown in Figure 15-3.**

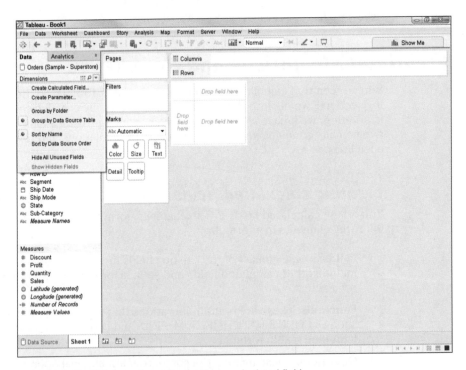

Figure 15-3: Use this menu to begin creating a calculated field.

3. **Enter a name for the calculated field in the text box at the top of the dialog box, as shown in Figure 15-4.**

   Be sure to use a descriptive name, because this is the name that will appear in the list of fields in the Data pane.

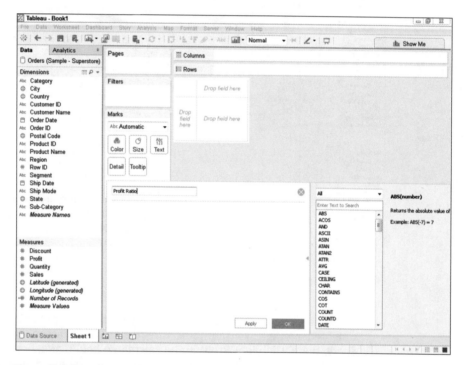

Figure 15-4: Enter a name that describes the field.

4. **Add the fields that you want to use in the formula by dragging and dropping the field onto the dialog box. (Note that you can also start typing the field name and then select the field from the list that appears.) Add operators by typing them in directly.**

   In this case, drag the Profit field onto the dialog box, then type the sign for division and add Sales after it, as shown in Figure 15-5.

5. **If you want to use any of the built-in functions in your formula, click the small arrow at the right side of the dialog box and then select the desired function from the list that appears.**

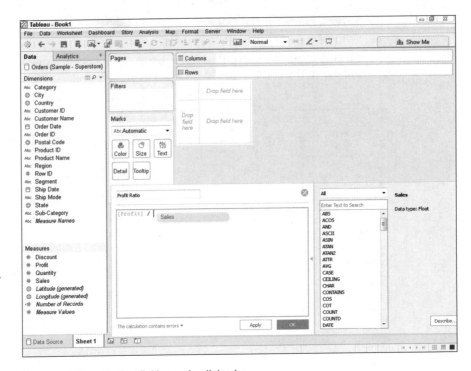

Figure 15-5: Drag the first field onto the dialog box.

In this case, because we are computing a profit ratio that requires a weighted average, we want to be sure to sum our measures before we divide them. Highlight Profit in the calculated field dialog box, and then click the arrow on the right to bring up the function list. Search for the aggregation of SUM and double-click. You'll notice that the aggregation gets put around the field with open and end parentheses. Do the same for Sales, as shown in Figure 15-6.

6. **Click OK to finish creating the calculated field, as shown in Figure 15-7.**

   When you click OK, Tableau adds it to the list of fields in the Data pane, and you can then use the calculated field in your views or in other calculations.

Tableau refers to the dialog box shown in this example as the *Equation Editor*. The name never appears in the dialog box, so you'll be forgiven if you just think of it as the dialog box where you create formulas.

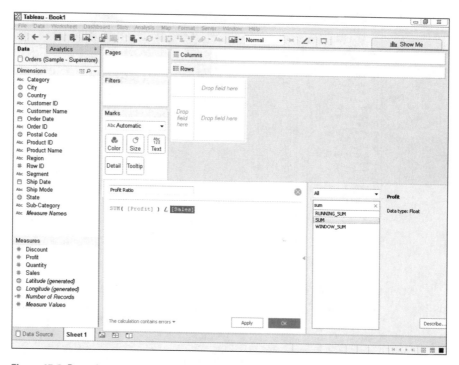

Figure 15-6: Drag the second field onto the dialog box and drop it after the operator.

Creating table calculations and percentages

Tableau offers a couple of different ways to add table calculations and percentages to the view. In most cases, you'll probably choose to use the very convenient quick table calculations to look at things like running total, percent of total, and year-over-year growth.

However, we'll take a different approach to creating a table calculation in order to show you all your options.

To add a table calculation, follow these steps:

1. **Build your view so that it contains a measure.**

2. **Click the down arrow on the measure to display its pop-up menu, as shown in Figure 15-8.**

3. **Choose Add Table Calculation from the pop-up menu.**

   Doing so displays the Table Calculation dialog box. You could use the Quick Table Calculation in many cases, but this example shows the steps you'd need to carry out in order to add the calculations and define how it's being computed.

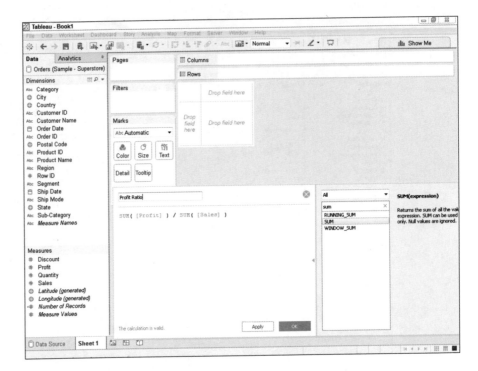

Figure 15-7: Click OK to finish.

4. **Choose the type of calculation you want from the Calculation Type list box, as shown in Figure 15-9.**

5. **Select the additional options to define the calculation, as shown in Figure 15-10.**

   The available options differ depending on the type of calculation you're adding to the view.

6. **After you've made your selections, click OK, as shown in Figure 15-11.**

   Figure 15-12 shows how the view appears after the table calculation has been added. Notice that Tableau indicates that the visualization contains a null value (the indicators in the lower-right corner of the view). This null value is the result of using a table calculation that shows the difference from the previous value. Because the first value in the view doesn't have a previous value to compare with, the result is null, as expected.

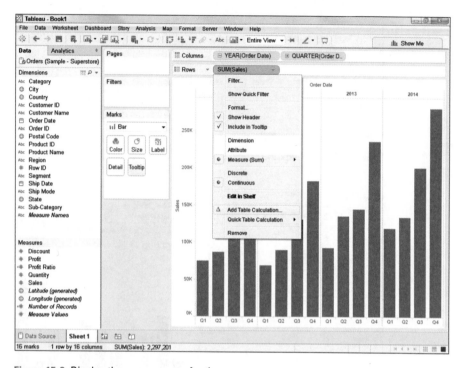

Figure 15-8: Display the pop-up menu for the measure.

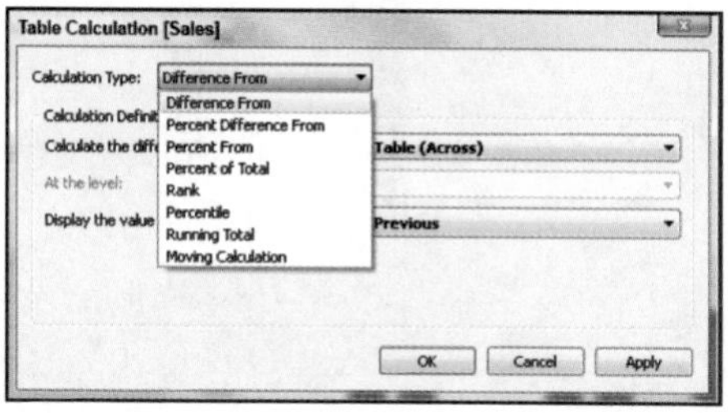

Figure 15-9: Choose your calculation type.

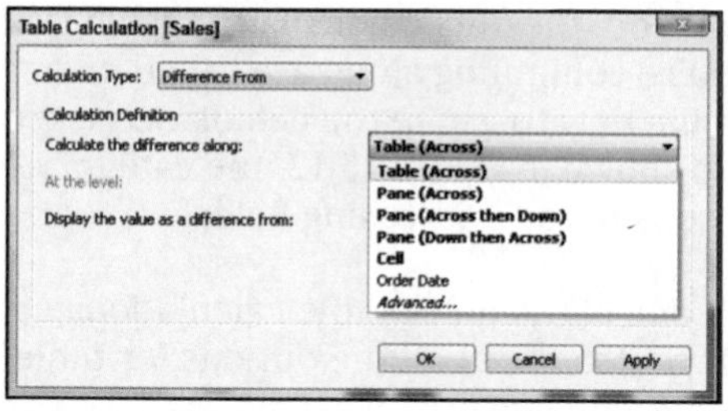

Figure 15-10: Choose your options.

Figure 15-11: Complete the process.

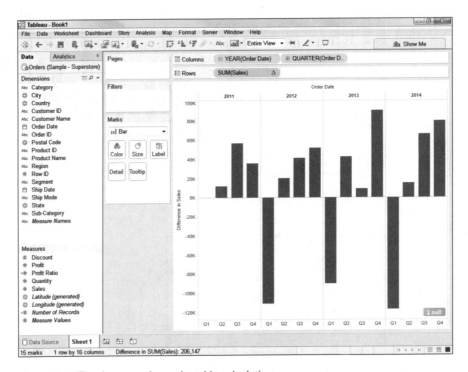

Figure 15-12: The view now shows the table calculation.

When you add a table calculation, the dimensions in the table that define the section on the table that you're computing along are called *addressing* fields, and the dimensions that define how to group the calculation are called *partitioning* fields. In the example shown in Figure 15-12, the category/region fields span the table, so they are considered addressing fields.

It's usually easier to choose one of the quick table calculations using the default values rather than trying to select all the options for table calculations using the Table Calculation dialog box.

Percentages are a specialized type of table calculation that shows the analysis as percentages rather than numeric values. Figure 15-13 shows the options that appear when you choose Analysis ➪ Percentage Of from Tableau's main menu.

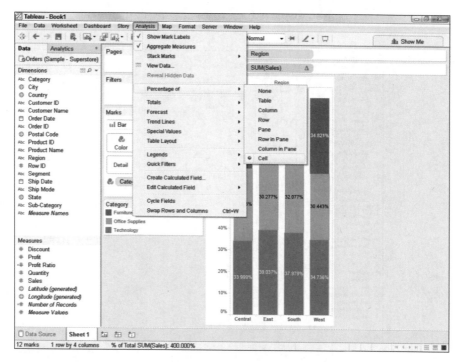

Figure 15-13: Your choices for displaying percentage calculations.

If you make a selection of a different type of table calculation such as a percentage, your existing table calculation is replaced. If you want to keep both types of views, make sure that you use the Duplicate Sheet button on the main toolbar to make a copy of the worksheet where you can choose a new type of calculation for the view.

Creating parameters

Parameters are values that you can use in things like bins, calculations, filters, and reference lines. Unlike fixed values, however, parameters can be selected and changed by those interacting with your visualizations. For example, suppose that you'd like to create a view that projects future sales based upon choosing a growth rate percentage compared to existing sales. You'd like to give several options so that an executive can see exactly how the different growth rates would affect sales.

To create a parameter in this example, follow these steps:

1. **Click the down arrow to the right of Dimensions in the Data pane and select Create Parameter from the pop-up menu that appears, as shown in Figure 15-14.**

   Doing so displays the Create Parameter dialog box.

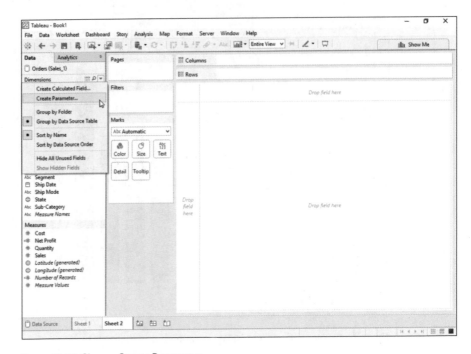

Figure 15-14: Choose Create Parameter.

2. **Enter a descriptive name for the parameter in the dialog box's Name field, as shown in Figure 15-15.**

3. **Select a data type from the Data Type drop-down menu, as shown in Figure 15-16.**

   In this case, Float is a good choice because you want to have the parameter specify a decimal value.

4. **Enter the default value for the parameter in the Current Value field, as shown in Figure 15-17.**

   In this case, .05 represents 5 percent, the minimum growth rate that you want to use in your view.

Figure 15-15: Enter a name that describes the parameter.

Figure 15-16: Choose the data type for the parameter.

Figure 15-17: Enter a default value.

5. **Choose the display format, as shown in Figure 15-18.**

   In this example, you want the format to be Percentage with 0 decimal places.

6. **Finally, specify the allowable values, as shown in Figure 15-19.**

   For this example, you want to use a range of values with a minimum of 5 percent, a maximum of 20 percent, and steps at each 5 percent between the minimum and maximum.

7. **Click OK to finish creating the parameter.**

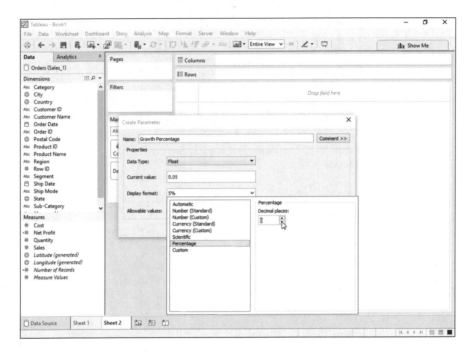

Figure 15-18: Select a format.

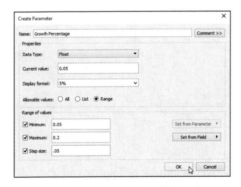

Figure 15-19: Specify the allowable values.

Customizing Your Data with Parameters

Earlier sections in this chapter show you how to create calculated fields and parameters. This last section shows that you can put both of them to use in a view. In this case, we'll use the Growth Percentage parameter to create a visualization that shows the projected sales that result from choosing different values for the parameter.

To create this example, follow these steps:

1. **Create a new calculated field named Projected Sales by entering the formula in the Equation Editor, as shown in Figure 15-20.**

   Refer to the "Creating calculated fields" section, earlier in this chapter, for more on creating calculated fields.

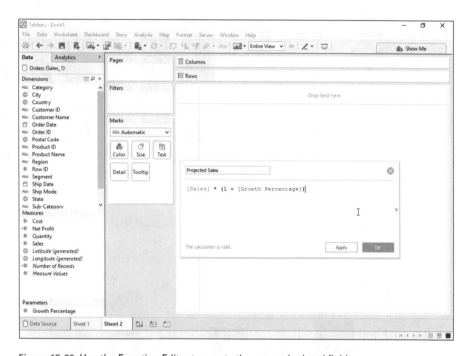

Figure 15-20: Use the Equation Editor to create the new calculated field.

2. **Add the Sales and Projected Sales measures to the view on the Rows shelf.**

3. **Add Category to the view on the Columns shelf.**

4. **Click the arrow at the right side of the Growth Percentage parameter to display its pop-up menu, as shown in Figure 15-21.**

5. **Choose the Show Parameter Control option on the menu to display the control so that it can be used to select values for the parameter in the view.**

   Figure 15-22 shows how the parameter control can be used to select different growth percentages to display in the view.

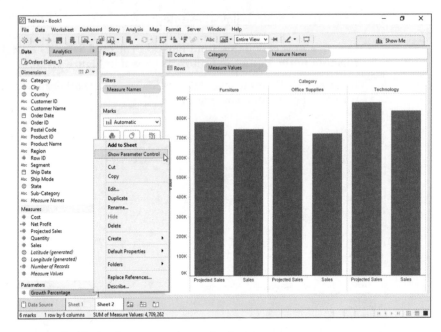

Figure 15-21: Display the contextual menu for the parameter.

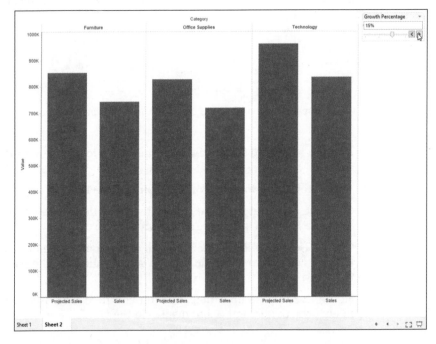

Figure 15-22: The parameter control enables you to select the growth percentage to display.

Percentage
Decimal places:

Percentage
Decimal places:

Percentage
Decimal places:

Percentage
Decimal places:

16

Percentage
Decimal places:

Percentage
Decimal places:

Percentage
Decimal places:

Percentage
Decimal places:

Percentage
Decimal places:

Unlocking the Language of Calculated Fields

In This Chapter

▶ Understanding data types

▶ Using built-in functions

▶ Looking at operators

C alculated fields give you the power to do some pretty amazing things in Tableau. Making full use of calculated fields is much easier when you understand what's possible, so this chapter provides the information that you need to know. Don't worry; we're not going to turn this into some deeply technical (and boring) exhaustive programming reference. Rather, we'll give you a feeling for the elements that you can use in Tableau's calculations.

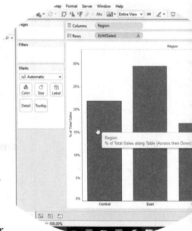

Looking at Data Types

Just as the fields in a database each have a specific data type, Tableau depends upon having your data fall into specific data types. This requirement is especially true when that data is used in a calculation. For example, if you're doing a calculation that involves dates, the data that you supply needs to be valid as a date.

In many cases, you can convert data from one type to another, but that does involve an extra step. Just remember that keeping your data type ducks in a row is important when using Tableau.

Tableau supports the following data types in calculations:

- **Boolean:** This data type can hold the values `true` and `false`.

- **Date/Datetime:** This data type can help to leverage Tableau's default date hierarchy behavior when applied to valid date or datetime fields.

- **Number:** These are values that are numeric. Number values can be integers or floating-point numbers (numbers with decimals).

- **String:** These are a sequence of characters enclosed in either single or double quotation marks.

Understanding Functions

Functions are pieces of built-in programming in Tableau that enable you to manipulate data in various ways. If you've used Excel, you're no doubt familiar with the functions that you use in formulas, such as `=SUM()`. Tableau includes many functions that work exactly like those you find in Excel (although in Tableau you don't need to include the `=` preceding the function name). Of course, the built-in functions in Tableau also include a number that are used for specific purposes that you won't find in Excel.

Tableau's functions fall into the following categories:

- **Number functions:** These are functions that you use to manipulate numeric values. For example, finding the sum of a set of numbers or determining the maximum value in a set would be number functions.

- **String functions:** You use these functions for working with string values. For example, you can use a string function to determine whether a specific string is located within a field.

- **Date functions:** These are functions that you use to work with dates and times. One example would be to determine the date when a product warranty expires based on the specified number of days after purchase.

- **Type conversion functions:** You use these functions to change data from one type to another. For example, you can convert a string that looks like a date into a date value that's valid for use in calculations.

- **Logical functions:** These are functions that enable you to test values and then control what Tableau does based upon those values. For example, you can return one result for sales that meet your targets and a different result for sales that fall below the target.

- **Aggregate functions:** These are functions that enable you to perform mathematical aggregations, such as finding the average value or the maximum value in a field.

✓ **Pass-through functions:** These are specialized functions that enable you to send SQL commands directly to a database. Most users won't ever use these types of functions, but Tableau includes them so that you can leverage database query functionality that Tableau might not inherently have.

✓ **User functions:** These are functions specific to Tableau Server or Tableau Online that enable you to control who can see certain data when the view is published. For example, you can make sure that sales reps can only see their own sales data in views that you publish.

✓ **Table calculation functions:** These are functions that enable you to customize how table calculations work. One example would be to limit the number of rows that are used in a calculation.

✓ **Additional functions:** These are more specialized functions that may, for example, be used with certain large data sources such as Hadoop and Google BigQuery. For example, one such additional function converts a UNIX timestamp into a date value that Tableau can use.

Considering Operators

Operators are the elements of a formula that tell Tableau how to process the various pieces of the formula. For example, a + means that the values should be added together. Operators include more than simply mathematical symbols. They also can include symbols like < (less than) and > (greater than) for comparing values and words like NOT and OR to control logical operations.

Tableau evaluates operators in a specific order. If your calculations don't seem to be producing the expected results, you might want to use parentheses to control the order of operation. That's because Tableau evaluates equations based on the nesting of parentheses, working from the deepest level outward.

Part VI

The Part of Tens

Enjoy an additional Part of Tens chapter online at: www.dummies.com/extras/tableau.

In this part . . .

- ✔ Discover ten great Tableau tips.
- ✔ Investigate ten great Tableau resources.

17

Ten Great Tableau Tips

In This Chapter

▶ Ten tips to remember when using Tableau

*W*e wouldn't be doing our job if we didn't share some tips to help you get the most from Tableau. This brief chapter provides some ideas that you'll want to remember.

Don't Wait for Your Source Data to Be Perfect

Tableau can even help you to discover where you have dirty data. You can use Tableau to understand your data issues quickly, and then make the necessary changes to your underlying data when you have more time or resources.

Reuse Data Connections

When connecting to data, there is a method that allows you to use a connection from another workbook. Choose the Other Files option from the Connect pane, and then select the workbook with the data source that you would like to use in the new workbook. If you use Tableau Server or Tableau Online, you have even more scalable and secure options for sharing data connections!

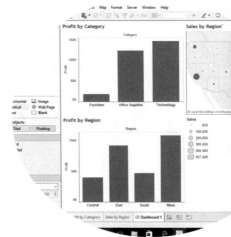

When in Doubt, Right-Click

You can find so many options in menus that Tableau opens as needed — try right-clicking and exploring.

The Undo Button Is Your Friend

If you ever get yourself into a tight spot, Tableau's unlimited Undo feature will help get you to a place of peace. So don't be afraid to play with options in Tableau. The Undo button is always just a click away!

Pay Attention to Visual Cues

Tableau provides indicators to help as you conduct your analysis. For example, the Sort icons on dimensions and axes or "=" signs next to calculated fields in your Data pane.

Leverage Your Previous Work

Not only can you copy worksheets from one workbook to another, but you can also copy whole dashboards between workbooks! Simply right-click on the tab of the worksheet or dashboard you want to copy and select Copy Worksheet from the menu that appears. Then right-click over the tab area of your destination workbook and select Paste Worksheet.

Visual Best Practices Are Worth Learning

Designing for yourself is great, but take a step back and ask yourself "Would this view make sense to anyone other than me?" There's tons of great information on visual best practices available, including www.tableau.com/learn/whitepapers/tableau-visual-guidebook.

Test for Performance

When you're considering sharing your work, double-check the speed and ease of interactivity you have designed. Even if the insight is worth the wait, slow dashboards are not fun for busy users. Search Tableau's white papers for information on improving workbook performance. The following is a good place to start: www.tableau.com/learn/whitepapers/designing-efficient-workbooks.

Keep It Simple

It's easy to get excited and overcomplicate your analysis with complex views and intricate details that can confuse your message. Your work should answer a question or two — but not every question that needs an answer.

Save Early and Often

But you knew that!

18

Ten Tableau Resources

*I*t really wouldn't be possible to cover everything there is to know about Tableau in a single book, so in this chapter we're going to show you some great places where you can find out just a bit more.

Free On-Demand Training

What's better than free? As Figure 18-1 shows, you can find great free Tableau training at `www.tableau.com/learn/training?qt-training_tabs=1`.

In-Person and Virtual Classroom Training

Want some more hands-on training? Look no further than `www.tableau.com/learn/training?qt-training_tabs=3`, as shown in Figure 18-2. Training is offered at a variety of locations, with a variety of levels of depth, and provides tons of opportunities to get your hands dirty with the product.

Community and Forums

Sometimes the best help comes from discussions with other users. Tableau has an active online user community at `http://community.tableau.com`, as shown in Figure 18-3. Many local communities also offer customer-led Tableau user groups where you can meet other Tableau users in your area.

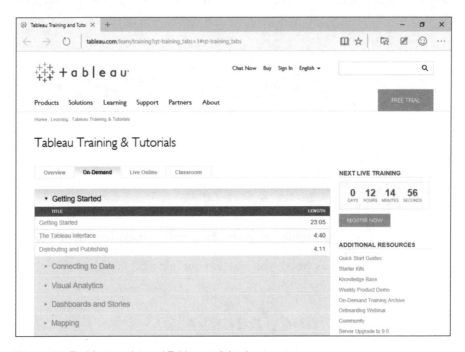

Figure 18-1: Find free on-demand Tableau training here.

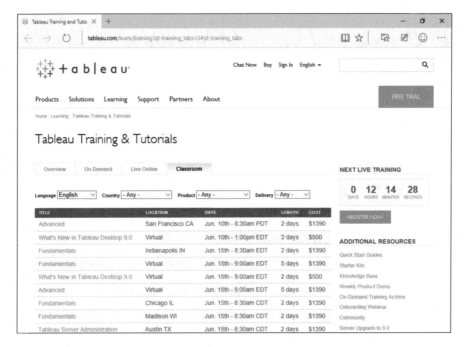

Figure 18-2: Find hands-on Tableau training here.

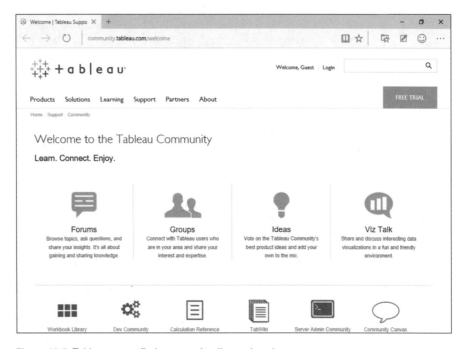

Figure 18-3: Tableau users find community discussions here.

Knowledge Base

Tableau maintains a very useful knowledge base where you can find tons of information. You can find it at `http://kb.tableau.com`, as shown in Figure 18-4.

Support

Want some inside help? Try Tableau Support at `www.tableau.com/support/product`, as shown in Figure 18-5.

Tableau Visual Gallery

Need some ideas about what you can do with Tableau? Have a look at the examples at `www.tableau.com/learn/gallery`, as shown in Figure 18-6.

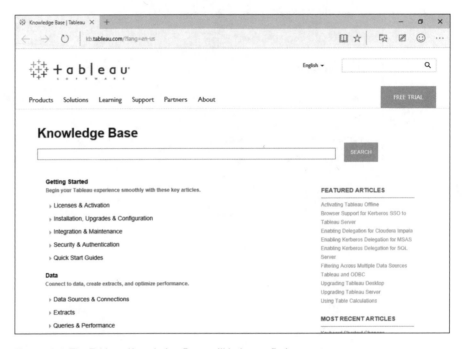

Figure 18-4: The Tableau Knowledge Base will help you find answers.

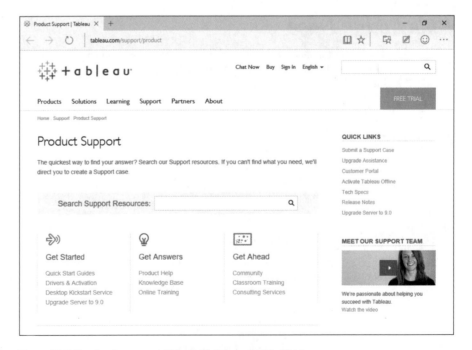

Figure 18-5: Here's where you will find official support for Tableau.

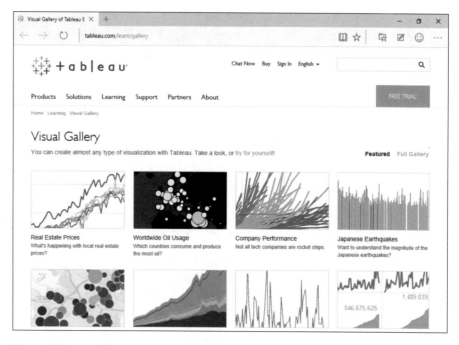

Figure 18-6: Here's a great place to see what Tableau can do.

White Papers

White papers are a great resource, especially when you need to explain why Tableau is right for your company. See www.tableau.com/learn/whitepapers, as shown in Figure 18-7, to find them.

On-Demand and Live Webinars

Webinars provide knowledge direct from the experts. Find them at www.tableau.com/learn/webinars, as shown in Figure 18-8.

Events and Conferences

Want to go to a Tableau event to learn more about the product and connect with other users? Find an event in your area at www.tableau.com/learn/events, as shown in Figure 18-9.

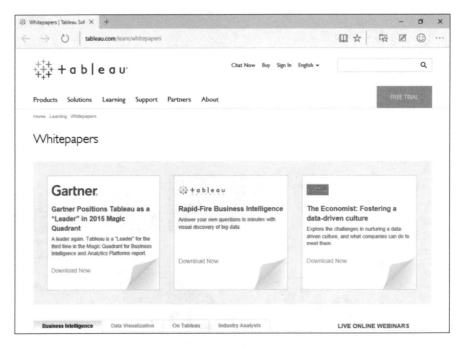

Figure 18-7: Tableau offers great white papers here.

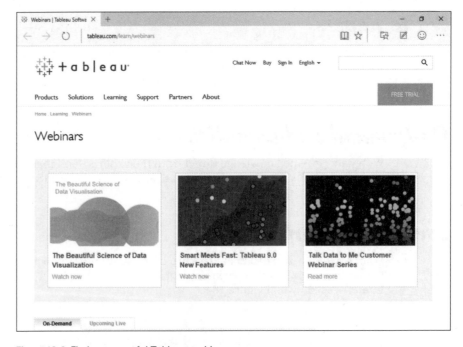

Figure 18-8: Find many useful Tableau webinars.

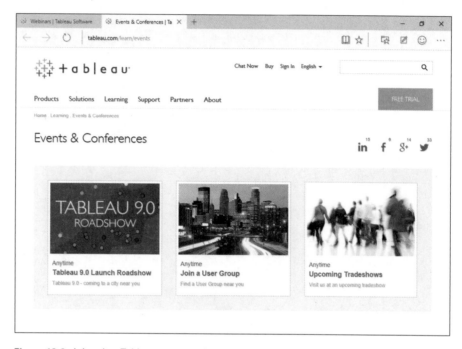

Figure 18-9: Join other Tableau users at these events.

Tableau-Related Blogs

But wait, there's more! You'll also want to check out some great data visualization blogs (thanks to Andy Kriebel of VizWiz):

- **Zen Masters:** `http://vizwiz.blogspot.com/p/cool-data-viz-blogs.html`

- **Facebook pages:** `http://vizwiz.blogspot.com/p/facebook-pages.html`

- **Data Viz blogs:** `http://vizwiz.blogspot.com/p/data-viz-blogs.html`

Index

• B •

• *U* •

• *V* •

About the Authors

Molly Monsey joined Tableau in 2009 as a technical product consultant, after spending time as an accounting analyst, also bringing prior experience in sales, training, and analytics. In 2011, she joined Paul Sochan to help build the training team at Tableau and together they set out to develop and deliver educational offerings around the world. They started the Train the Trainer program and Molly began successfully recruiting, training, and supporting instructors who educate Tableau users all over the world. She now leads members of the training team charged with managing training product offerings globally, including developing content and enabling internal and external resources. Molly is a Seattle native, a graduate of the University of Washington Business School, and is also a member of the infamous Tableau company band, Dragged and Dropped.

Paul Sochan joined Tableau in 2010 and serves as the Senior Director of Global Education Services. Paul was the first member of the training team at Tableau, and was responsible for developing and delivering the first Tableau education offerings. Molly joined Paul on the training team in 2011, and together they have built a team to develop and deliver training curriculum on Tableau Desktop and Tableau Server globally.

Paul has an extensive background in Business Intelligence, having started in the space in 1994 as an early employee at Crystal Decisions, makers of Crystal Reports. Since that time, Paul has spent over 20 years educating and evangelizing best practices in turning data into decision-making information in a number of roles.

Paul earned a Bachelor of Engineering and Bachelor of Arts from the University of Waterloo and a Master in Economics from McMaster University in Canada and currently resides in Seattle with his wife and four children.

Dedication

I dedicate this book to my family. They are forced to tolerate my crazy hours of work and obsession with all that is Tableau. My wife Wendy Bolf, and my children Lydia Sochan, Melanie Herbin, Jeremy Herbin, and Natalya Sochan. Please realize that my data query sorted your names based on age and no other factor. I adore you all!!!

— Paul Sochan

Publisher's Acknowledgments

Acquisitions Editor: Amy Fandrei

Senior Project Editor: Paul Levesque

Copy Editor: John Edwards

Editorial Assistant: Bridget Feeney

Sr. Editorial Assistant: Cherie Case

Project Coordinator: Antony Sami

Cover Image: Sergey Nivens/Shutterstock

Apple & Mac

iPad For Dummies,
5th Edition
978-1-118-72306-7

iPhone For Dummies,
7th Edition
978-1-118-69083-3

Macs All-in-One
For Dummies, 4th Edition
978-1-118-82210-4

OS X Mavericks
For Dummies
978-1-118-69188-5

Blogging & Social Media

Facebook For Dummies,
5th Edition
978-1-118-63312-0

Social Media Engagement
For Dummies
978-1-118-53019-1

WordPress For Dummies,
6th Edition
978-1-118-79161-5

Business

Stock Investing
For Dummies, 4th Edition
978-1-118-37678-2

Investing For Dummies,
6th Edition
978-0-470-90545-6

Personal Finance
For Dummies, 7th Edition
978-1-118-11785-9

QuickBooks 2014
For Dummies
978-1-118-72005-9

Small Business Marketing
Kit For Dummies,
3rd Edition
978-1-118-31183-7

Careers

Job Interviews
For Dummies, 4th Edition
978-1-118-11290-8

Job Searching with Social
Media For Dummies,
2nd Edition
978-1-118-67856-5

Personal Branding
For Dummies
978-1-118-11792-7

Resumes For Dummies,
6th Edition
978-0-470-87361-8

Starting an Etsy Business
For Dummies, 2nd Edition
978-1-118-59024-9

Diet & Nutrition

Belly Fat Diet For Dummies
978-1-118-34585-6

Mediterranean Diet
For Dummies
978-1-118-71525-3

Nutrition For Dummies,
5th Edition
978-0-470-93231-5

Digital Photography

Digital SLR Photography
All-in-One For Dummies,
2nd Edition
978-1-118-59082-9

Digital SLR Video &
Filmmaking For Dummies
978-1-118-36598-4

Photoshop Elements 12
For Dummies
978-1-118-72714-0

Gardening

Herb Gardening
For Dummies, 2nd Edition
978-0-470-61778-6

Gardening with Free-Range
Chickens For Dummies
978-1-118-54754-0

Health

Boosting Your Immunity
For Dummies
978-1-118-40200-9

Diabetes For Dummies,
4th Edition
978-1-118-29447-5

Living Paleo For Dummies
978-1-118-29405-5

Big Data

Big Data For Dummies
978-1-118-50422-2

Data Visualization
For Dummies
978-1-118-50289-1

Hadoop For Dummies
978-1-118-60755-8

Language &
Foreign Language

500 Spanish Verbs
For Dummies
978-1-118-02382-2

English Grammar
For Dummies, 2nd Edition
978-0-470-54664-2

French All-in-One
For Dummies
978-1-118-22815-9

German Essentials
For Dummies
978-1-118-18422-6

Italian For Dummies,
2nd Edition
978-1-118-00465-4

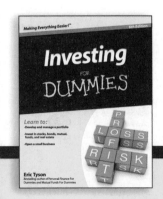 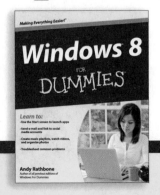  

Available in print and e-book formats.

Available wherever books are sold. **For more information or to order direct visit www.dummies.com**

Math & Science

Algebra I For Dummies,
2nd Edition
978-0-470-55964-2

Anatomy and Physiology
For Dummies, 2nd Edition
978-0-470-92326-9

Astronomy For Dummies,
3rd Edition
978-1-118-37697-3

Biology For Dummies,
2nd Edition
978-0-470-59875-7

Chemistry For Dummies,
2nd Edition
978-1-118-00730-3

1001 Algebra II Practice
Problems For Dummies
978-1-118-44662-1

Microsoft Office

Excel 2013 For Dummies
978-1-118-51012-4

Office 2013 All-in-One
For Dummies
978-1-118-51636-2

PowerPoint 2013
For Dummies
978-1-118-50253-2

Word 2013 For Dummies
978-1-118-49123-2

Music

Blues Harmonica
For Dummies
978-1-118-25269-7

Guitar For Dummies,
3rd Edition
978-1-118-11554-1

iPod & iTunes
For Dummies, 10th Edition
978-1-118-50864-0

Programming

Beginning Programming
with C For Dummies
978-1-118-73763-7

Excel VBA Programming
For Dummies, 3rd Edition
978-1-118-49037-2

Java For Dummies,
6th Edition
978-1-118-40780-6

Religion & Inspiration

The Bible For Dummies
978-0-7645-5296-0

Buddhism For Dummies,
2nd Edition
978-1-118-02379-2

Catholicism For Dummies,
2nd Edition
978-1-118-07778-8

Self-Help & Relationships

Beating Sugar Addiction
For Dummies
978-1-118-54645-1

Meditation For Dummies,
3rd Edition
978-1-118-29144-3

Seniors

Laptops For Seniors
For Dummies, 3rd Edition
978-1-118-71105-7

Computers For Seniors
For Dummies, 3rd Edition
978-1-118-11553-4

iPad For Seniors
For Dummies, 6th Edition
978-1-118-72826-0

Social Security
For Dummies
978-1-118-20573-0

Smartphones & Tablets

Android Phones
For Dummies, 2nd Edition
978-1-118-72030-1

Nexus Tablets
For Dummies
978-1-118-77243-0

Samsung Galaxy S 4
For Dummies
978-1-118-64222-1

Samsung Galaxy Tabs
For Dummies
978-1-118-77294-2

Test Prep

ACT For Dummies,
5th Edition
978-1-118-01259-8

ASVAB For Dummies,
3rd Edition
978-0-470-63760-9

GRE For Dummies,
7th Edition
978-0-470-88921-3

Officer Candidate Tests
For Dummies
978-0-470-59876-4

Physician's Assistant Exam
For Dummies
978-1-118-11556-5

Series 7 Exam For Dummies
978-0-470-09932-2

Windows 8

Windows 8.1 All-in-One
For Dummies
978-1-118-82087-2

Windows 8.1 For Dummies
978-1-118-82121-3

Windows 8.1 For Dummies,
Book + DVD Bundle
978-1-118-82107-7

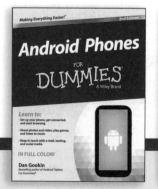

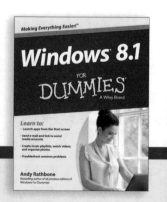

Take Dummies with you everywhere you go!

Whether you are excited about e-books, want more from the web, must have your mobile apps, or are swept up in social media, Dummies makes everything easier.

...e the Power

For Dummies is the global leader in the reference category and one of the most trusted and highly regarded brands in the world. No longer just focused on books, customers now have access to the For Dummies content they need in the format they want. Let us help you develop a solution that will fit your brand and help you connect with your customers.

Advertising & Sponsorships

Connect with an engaged audience on a powerful multimedia site, and position your message alongside expert how-to content.

Targeted ads • Video • Email marketing • Microsites • Sweepstakes sponsorship

21 Million Monthly Page Views & 13 Million Unique Visitors